On Niccolò Machiavelli

CORE KNOWLEDGE

CORE KNOWLEDGE

The Core Knowledge series takes its motivation from the goals, ideals, challenges, and pleasures of Columbia College's Core Curriculum. The aim is to capture the intellectual energy and the stimulus to creative thinking that is a fundamental ideal of such courses as Literature Humanities and Contemporary Civilization. In the spirit of Core teaching, the books are intended to reflect on what the featured works can be if approached from different or unusual vantage points; how they may inform modern experience; and how they are to be viewed not as sources of plain fact, certainty, and assured beliefs but as provocations to the imagination that help us to see differently, experimentally, and with a spirit of intellectual adventure.

PUBLISHED IN THE CORE KNOWLEDGE SERIES

On Ovid's Metamorphoses, Gareth Williams

On John Stuart Mill, Philip Kitcher

On Mary Wollstonecraft's A Vindication of the Rights of Woman: A New Genre, Susan J. Wolfson

On
Niccolò
Machiavelli

The Bonds of Politics

Gabriele Pedullà

Columbia University Press / *New York*

Columbia University Press
Publishers Since 1893
New York   Chichester, West Sussex
cup.columbia.edu

Library of Congress Cataloging-in-Publication Data
Names: Pedullà, Gabriele, author.
Title: On Niccolò Machiavelli : the bonds of politics / Gabriele
    Pedullà.
Description: New York : Columbia University Press, [2024] |
    Series: Core knowledge | Includes bibliographical references
    and index.
Identifiers: LCCN 2023012056 (print) | LCCN 2023012057 (ebook) |
    ISBN 9780231205542 (hardback) | ISBN 9780231205559
    (trade paperback) | ISBN 9780231556057 (ebook)
Subjects: LCSH: Machiavelli, Niccolò, 1469–1527.
Classification: LCC JC143.M4 P43 2024 (print) | LCC JC143.M4
    (ebook) | DDC 320.1092 [B]—dc23/eng/20230329
LC record available at https://lccn.loc.gov/2023012056
LC ebook record available at https://lccn.loc.gov/2023012057

Printed in the United States of America

Cover design: Lisa Hamm
Cover image: *Niccolò di Bernardo dei Machiavelli*. Portrait by
Santi di Tito. Archive/Alamy Stock Photo.

To Nicola Di Cosmo and Francesca Trivellato,
with special affection and gratitude

Contents

Preface: The Thinker of a Thousand Faces

Every day I discover in you a greater prophet than the Jews or any other people ever had.

—Filippo Casavecchia to Niccolò Machiavelli, June 17, 1509

Who was Niccolò Machiavelli? Even today, scholars do not agree: indeed, it can be said that no Western political thinker has ever been described in as many contradictory ways. Was he a friend of tyrants, as a centuries-old "black legend" affirms? Did he commit himself to the Medici house at a certain point of his life, or did he remain faithful to the republican institutions of his native Florence? Did he inaugurate a realistic politics, interested in describing men "as they are" instead of "as they should be"? Or was he the first to separate politics from ethics and religion, as people began to say in the aftermath of the French Revolution? Did he anticipate the rise of the modern state in its struggle against feudal powers (another idea that arose in the same crucial years)? Or did he inspire power politics and twentieth-century totalitarianism? Was he the "Galileo of social studies," the theorist of a scientific and ultimately "technified" politics? Or, rather, should we recognize in him a great builder of political myths, capable of communicating his ideas through memorable images (the centaur Chiron, half-man and half-horse, who instructed the greatest princes of Greece; Fortune-woman, who must be "beaten" by impetuous politicians; the banks of Virtue that contain the river Fortune . . .)? Was his aim the welfare of the whole community? Or was he just a champion of the people against the Florentine financial oligarchy? Can he be hailed as the prophet of Italian national unity? Or should we celebrate him as the most original modern theorist of mixed government, whose pages were pondered by the Founding Fathers when they drafted the American Constitution? Was he completely skeptical about Christianity? Or should we instead value his reflections on the importance of a civil religion that guarantees— through the fear of divine punishment—respect for oaths? And what about the maxim that "the ends justify the means," which many credit him with—even if it cannot be found in any of his works and was instead a famous Jesuit motto ("when the ends are good, the means are good too")?

The following pages will try to answer these questions. For now, as a preamble, just a couple of preliminary points are to be made. In many respects, Machiavelli deserves appreciation as a precursor and innovator, even an iconoclast—but this is just part of the story. In a time when the new classicizing culture of the humanists distinguished Italy from the other European countries, his first-rate education put him in the position of managing countless Roman and Greek sources (in Latin translation), and even if he would eventually oppose humanist political theory in his works, he never stopped looking for inspiration from the ancients (an approach very different from that of Thomas Hobbes, the other presumptive "father" of political modernity).

From this point of view, Machiavelli resembles the mythical Janus, the Roman god of openings and endings, who was represented with two faces, one looking into the past and the other into the future.

Another contrast, however, seems no less useful in describing Machiavelli's place in Western political thought—that between mainstream and fringe thinkers. Curiously enough, Machiavelli has been both (and sometimes simultaneously!) firmly rooted at the center of the canon and glaringly misunderstood or read only in fragments. If ideology is like an unbreakable and invisible pane of glass, Machiavelli is one of the few authors who had the very rare gift of identifying the pressure points that shatter it—and it is above all this ability to swim against the current that deserves to be highlighted when we read him. For, as his friend Francesco Guicciardini once acknowledged in a letter, Machiavelli was an "inventor of new and unusual things" who "had always extravagant opinions" (May 18, 1521).

Such outspoken nonconformism never won Machiavelli many friends, and sometimes he paid heavily for it. The uneven reception of his most daring ideas is, however, precisely one of the reasons why they remain so relevant today—provided that, in the true spirit of the Core Knowledge series, one frees them from the simplistic formulas that so often have been imposed upon *The Prince* and the *Discourses on Livy* in the last two centuries. In order to understand an author like Machiavelli, whose writings immediately caused a stir among his contemporaries, one must therefore start from the historical context in which his works took shape and created a sensation.

Hence, in presenting his thought I will place particular emphasis on two issues. First, I will dwell on the (conventional and unconventional) forms with which he conveyed his ideas. This is a pivotal point: we should think of Renaissance genres (and literary genres in general) not as a set of imperatives imposed on the authors but rather as the lenses through which they observe the world and organize their vision. This is especially true for Machiavelli. Not only did he renovate long-established literary forms of expression by introducing elements taken from other genres (in *The Art of War*, *The Mandrake*, and the *Florentine Histories*) but in one case he quietly subverted many of the unwritten rules of the traditional handbook for rulers (in *The Prince*), and in another he created ex novo a philosophical genre that was destined to impose itself throughout Europe for almost three centuries, eventually ushering in the birth of the modern essay (in the *Discourses on Livy*). The formal devices chosen by thinkers to present their ideas always matter, but they are even more noteworthy in the case of Machiavelli, who is also one of the great playwrights and, more generally, one of the great writers of Italian literature.

Second, I will try to bring to light the invisible threads that bind together all Machiavelli's works. A long tradition of interpretation has contrasted *The Prince* and the *Discourses*, seeing in the former a pro-principality treatise and in the latter a pro-republican one, and judging them somehow irreconcilable. Instead, well beyond Machiavelli's different investment in the two projects (the first, a brilliant piece of occasional writing, the second a wide-ranging and long-pondered general reassessment of what free governments are, how they work, and how they can last), the following pages will stress the profound continuity of his beliefs: his attention to social and political bonds, his fiercely antioligarchic stance, his appreciation for self-made leaders who

did not rely on family privilege in their ascent, his full awareness of the economic aspects of power relations (an uncommon
feature for his times), his constant focus on warfare (the real
touchstone of virtue), his strong preference for history over philosophy as a guide for politicians, and many more. Machiavelli
is celebrated today for his realism (or even considered to be the
father of political realism), and such realism undoubtedly implied
a high degree of adaptability to different situations. But carefully reading his works in their historical context will reveal the
extraordinary coherence of his project: from his origins as a
humanist in the making to his final years, when, after a rocky
and often difficult life, for a short time Machiavelli finally won
the public recognition he had long deserved.

I would like to thank Gareth Williams and Elisabeth Lad-
enson, who invited me to write this book for their series and who
never failed to support me during the editorial process; the Core
Knowledge Editorial Board; and the anonymous reviewers.
Their suggestions made these pages better. I also benefited from
the help of three competent friends who generously discussed
the whole manuscript with me: Giulio Azzolini, Jérémie Barthas,
and Yves Winter; Piero Innocenti and Marielisa Rossi provided
me with precious bibliographical information. Most of the text
was drafted in the spring of 2022, at the Institute for Advanced
Study in Princeton (where the welcoming ghosts of Felix Gilbert and Albert O. Hirschman often visited me during the
night). An initial version of the first three chapters was presented to the Early Modern Seminar run by Francesca Trivellato, who commented on it with her usual passion and expertise together with the other participants, especially Jérémie
Foa, Emily Kadens, Diana Kim, Peter Lake, and Robyn Marasco.

In March 2022 a first draft of chapter 3 was used as the basis for a lecture at Harvard upon Francesco Erspamer's invitation. Finally, I completed the final revisions at the University of California, in Berkeley, where I held the chair of Italian Culture during the spring semester of 2023 at the invitation of Mia Fuller; at that stage, some pages of the book were "tested" at the Italian Modernities Seminar at Stanford thanks to an invitation by Laura Wittmann. Patricia Gaborik and Brett Savage kindly checked and polished my English (Patricia more than once). I express my deepest gratitude to all of them.

On Niccolò Machiavelli

1

From Humanism to Politics

*To the greater sorrow and terror of men, the calamities
of Italy began at a time when the circumstances seemed
universally most propitious and fortunate.*

—Francesco Guicciardini, *History of Italy*

Paradise Lost

Niccolò Machiavelli belongs to one of those generations called
upon to confront a recent past regarded by everyone as exceptionally happy in comparison with a much harsher present. In
his case, the turning point came in 1494, when Machiavelli was
twenty-five years old and the king of France, Charles VIII,
crossed the Alps to claim his hereditary rights over the Kingdom of Naples, changing the setup of the peninsula for centuries. But the invasion triggered a veritable earthquake in Italians' minds too, and Machiavelli's works can only be understood
in light of such a major cultural, political, and existential shock.

For exactly forty years, Italy had enjoyed enviable stability.
As a result of the fear that the Ottoman conquest of Constan-
tinople (present-day Istanbul) had induced in Europe (1453), the
major Italian powers had subscribed to a general peace in Lodi

(1454), later joined by the Swiss. From that moment on, there were only occasional clashes, almost always fueled by the belligerent Sixtus IV (pope from 1471 to 1484), but, with the exception of Naples, the agreements held up extraordinarily well. This tranquility was all the more significant when compared to what was happening in other parts of Europe in the same years. The French monarchy had emerged victorious from the Hundred Years' War against England in 1453 only to find itself immediately involved in a series of struggles with the main feudal lords of the kingdom. More or less at the same time, England had been lacerated for thirty years by a civil war between the Houses of York and Lancaster (1455–1485). Spain was still divided into four distinct kingdoms, and when Ferdinand of Aragon and Isabella of Castile married, laying the foundations for the unification of the majority of the Iberian peninsula, the country was torn apart in bloody civil strife (1475–1479), after which the royal couple started a winning military campaign against the Kingdom of Granada, the last Islamic bulwark in Europe (1482–1492).

Formally, the medieval order persisted in Italy. Under the name of the Kingdom of Italy, the center-north (including Tuscany) was part of the Holy Roman Empire; the rest of central Italy was ruled by the church; and the Kingdom of Naples was considered a simple feudal vassal of the pontiff, just as the Kingdom of Sardinia was of the emperor. The only city-state officially independent of the two universal powers of the church and the empire was Venice, which in the ninth century had obtained full jurisdiction over the lagoon following an agreement between the Holy Roman and Byzantine emperors.

In reality, things were quite different, and the territory below the Alpine arcs was extremely fragmented. In addition to five major powers—the Duchy of Milan, the Republic of Venice, the

Republic of Florence, the Papal States, and the Kingdom of Naples—the Peace of Lodi recorded 115 minor political entities. In this polycentric framework, success had mainly smiled upon Venice, which since 1405 constantly increased its possessions on the mainland, the Terraferma (so called to distinguish it from the outposts in the Mediterranean that ensured the republic its lucrative trade with the East). Under the Visconti dynasty, on a couple of occasions, Milan had been on the point of aggregating a large state in the center-north, but the plan had always failed, and from 1450 the new Duke Francesco Sforza (linked to the Visconti by marriage) had refrained from attempting similar enterprises. From a military point of view, Florence was much less powerful, but the city had a vast commercial and financial network branching out across the continent and, thanks to its wealth, it was able to hire the most reputable mercenary commanders when necessary. The Papal States, on the other hand, paid for the lack of control over many of its territories (which the pope governed only nominally) and for the constant competition between the Roman feudal clans of the Orsini and Colonna, enemies in everything except their effort to limit the pontiff's authority. The Kingdom of Naples, finally, had passed from the French house d'Anjou to a cadet branch of the Aragonese of Spain after many vicissitudes that resulted in a devastating civil war (1435–1442), and it had eventually suffered two uprisings of the great nobility (1459–1464 and 1485–1486), which had further weakened it. The minor powers inserted themselves as best they could within this system of five: the lords of the small principalities in central Italy, for example, had specialized as mercenary commanders, and in this capacity they had achieved considerable resources by putting themselves at the service of the five major political players (figure 1.1).

Figure 1.1. Italy in 1494.

By eradicating internal conflict, the Peace of Lodi protected Italy from external interference, but fewer wars did not mean the end of the competition among the regional centers. The second half of the fifteenth century was therefore an age of spectacular conspiracies: in Rome (1453 and 1467), Naples (1459 and 1485), Milan (1476), and Florence (1478); only the aristocracy of Venice seemed immune. In short, open battles seem to have given way to secretive plots, according to a well-known stereotype about the perfidies of Renaissance Italy—a development that should be viewed instead as a side-effect of the successful efforts to contain armed conflicts and thus as a triumph of diplomacy. It is no surprise, therefore, that when they looked back on this prolonged era of peace at the beginning of the sixteenth century, some Florentine authors (like Bernando Rucellai, Francesco Guicciardini, and Machiavelli) coined the concept of the "balance of power," which in subsequent years would be applied increasingly to the entire European state system before becoming one of the bases of modern international relations.

Even in the absence of a unified state, people in the peninsula founded their idea of Italy and their feeling of common belonging on four criteria: physical (the territory south of the Alps), linguistic ("the beautiful country where the *sì* is heard," *Inferno* 33, v. 80), ethnic (the descendants of the Romans), and cultural (the true heirs of the classical tradition). Indeed, if in the Middle Ages it had been said that Italy was above all the seat of religious power (the papacy) while Germany had been given civil power (the empire) and France the learning of the universities, from the fourteenth century the revival of Greek and Roman culture promoted by the humanists was increasingly recognized as one of the main features that, regardless of the considerable differences across Italy's regions, distinguished their land from all other European countries.

During Machiavelli's childhood, this sense of affinity was also accompanied by an explicit feeling of superiority. As the Dutch humanist Erasmus of Rotterdam later lamented, Italians "have absorbed from pagan literature the mania for calling those who were born outside Italy barbarians. And this epithet, from them, is a graver insult than if you were to term them parricide or sacrilegious" (*Iulius exclusus e coelis*, 1514). However, such an attitude was not only proof of parochial arrogance. The first reason for pride was also the oldest and most obvious: Italy held the seat of the pontiff in Rome, who—besides being the guide of all Christians in spiritual matters—exercised an undisputed power of arbitration in conflicts between states all over Europe; just to give an example, in 1494 it was Pope Alexander VI who, through the Treaty of Tordesillas, established the boundaries of Spanish and Portuguese possessions in the lands recently conquered by Christopher Columbus and his followers in the Americas. The taxes that came to Rome from all over the continent (the "tithe") were thus only one of the many tangible signs of the church's ascendency in the temporal domain too.

Italy was also one of the richest and most urbanized countries in Europe (around one-quarter of its total population lived in the cities), especially in its central and northern regions, which, along with Flanders (present-day Belgium and Holland), had driven the continent's economy since at least the thirteenth century. This condition of widespread prosperity had been further enhanced in the fifteenth century as a result of forty years of peace; hence, in 1494, Italy could appear to French invaders as a land of unparalleled material well-being (and a rich prize for the taking). For instance, after his conquest of Naples, Charles VIII wrote to Peter II, duke of Bourbon, congratulating himself: "You could not believe the beautiful gardens that I possess in this city, for by my faith it seems that nothing is lacking except Adam and Eve to make them into an earthly paradise."

Moreover, having begun to explore ancient civilization in very original ways from the end of the thirteenth century, Italy also enjoyed an undisputed cultural primacy. This was attributable to the humanists' recovery of metrical forms and literary genres that had fallen into disuse and their assimilation of classical models in the arts. But at the same time they had also learned how to make use of the Greeks' and Romans' superior knowledge in fields such as medicine, botany, anatomy, geography, architecture, and astronomy and, more generally, in a great diversity of sciences and technical skills, which brought substantial practical benefits. This is the phenomenon, initially all Italian, that contemporaries described as a new "golden age" and that, less pompously, is today referred to as the Renaissance.

Lastly, despite the effectiveness of the 1454 agreements in preventing wars, the Italians believed they possessed one of the most powerful military systems in Europe. Not only were the peninsula's condottieri highly esteemed, but in the aftermath of the Peace of Lodi just three states on the entire continent had a stable army of considerable size, and two of them were in Italy: France (nine thousand men), Venice (eight thousand), and Milan (with a contingent just below that of Venice). Thus, when Charles VIII's invasion was imminent, the Milanese ambassador's dispatches reported that at that crucial juncture the only concern at the court of Naples was that the French sovereign could enlist Italian mercenaries, because only they were considered truly fearsome.

If Machiavelli grew up in such a seemingly stable world, the invasion of Charles VIII soon swept it away. The material damage of the incursions, the heavy taxation imposed by the occupiers, and the numerous plagues that hit Italy especially hard in the first decades of the sixteenth century little by little eroded the region's economic well-being, while the inability to resist the foreigners revealed the fragility of mercenary armies and spawned the idea that the Italians were cowards (as the French took to saying: "The Italians do not fight"). In light of the military defeats, even Italy's undisputed cultural achievements could be denounced as a sign of effete weakness (some suggested that this was just what had happened in Greece in the second century BCE, when the most advanced civilization in the Mediterranean basin was easily subjugated by the much less refined Romans). Only the pontiff's prestige remained unaffected by the general crisis—at least until 1517, when an obscure Augustinian friar from Germany, Martin Luther, attacked the corrupt customs of "New Babylon," thereby triggering the split of Christianity into two opposing camps, which would mark Europe's history for centuries to come. From the perspective of anyone born (like Machiavelli) in the second half of the fifteenth century, such a succession of calamities inevitably indicated the end of an entire world.

Revolution!

There was a complicated dynastic puzzle behind Charles VIII's expedition. From the thirteenth century, the Kingdom of Naples had been governed by the Angevins, who were closely related to the French royal family, but in 1442 it passed to the Aragonese of Spain. The local supporters of France did not give up, however, and, when in 1458 the old king Alfonso the Magnanimous bequeathed his Catalan possessions to his brother John II of Aragon and Naples to his illegitimate son Ferrante, part of the Neapolitan aristocracy rose up against Ferrante but was defeated after a long war. According to French propaganda, Charles VIII was therefore only reclaiming his legitimate right to the Neapolitan throne. Nevertheless, his real strength lay not in his family tree but in the riches that he drew from the very populous kingdom of France. Once the Hundred Years' War had ended, the taxes imposed to drive out the English invader had not been revoked, and the result was that the king of France became the first prince since the fall of the Roman Empire to benefit from a permanent tribute (that is, a form of taxation that was no longer granted by the subject communities on a case-by-case basis). Such a revenue stream put him in the unprecedented position of being able to plan a large-scale strategy, and Naples was Charles VIII's first target (figure 1.2).

In 1494, faced with the threat of invasion, instead of joining in a common league, the five main states of the peninsula split into many different fronts. While Florence confirmed its alliance with Naples, and Milan openly sided with France, Venice and the pope maintained an ambiguous attitude. In the absence of a unified answer from the Italians, for Charles VIII, who employed an army of unmatched size (over twenty thousand men) and equipped with powerful artillery, the expedition became a cakewalk. As the troops approached, Florence and the pope surrendered, and in February 1495, less than six months after crossing the Alps, the French sovereign entered Naples in

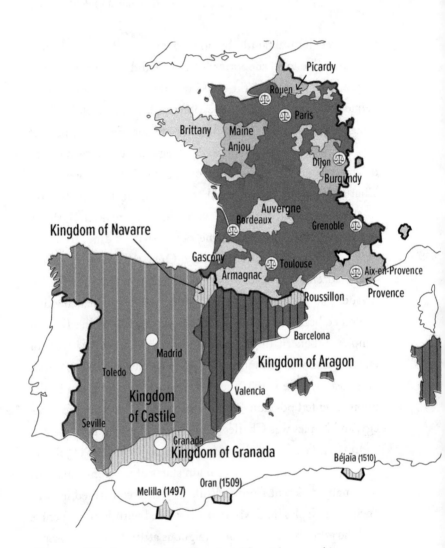

Figure 1.2. The formation of the French and Spanish monarchies (1469–1513).

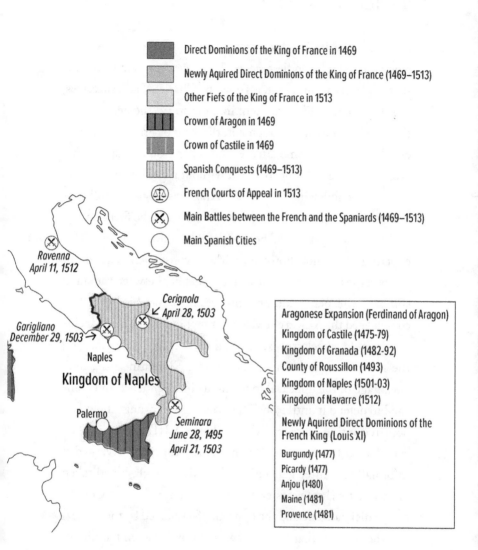

Direct Dominions of the King of France in 1469

Newly Aquired Direct Dominions of the King of France (1469–1513)

Other Fiefs of the King of France in 1513

Crown of Aragon in 1469

Crown of Castile in 1469

Spanish Conquests (1469–1513)

French Courts of Appeal in 1513

Main Battles between the French and the Spaniards (1469–1513)

Main Spanish Cities

Ravenna
April 11, 1512

Cerignola
April 28, 1503

Garigliano
December 29, 1503 →

Naples

Kingdom of Naples

Palermo

Seminara
June 28, 1495
April 21, 1503

Aragonese Expansion (Ferdinand of Aragon)

Kingdom of Castile (1475-79)
Kingdom of Granada (1482-92)
County of Roussillon (1493)
Kingdom of Naples (1501-03)
Kingdom of Navarre (1512)

Newly Aquired Direct Dominions of the
French King (Louis XI)

Burgundy (1477)
Picardy (1477)
Anjou (1480)
Maine (1481)
Provence (1481)

triumph. The Italians, accustomed as they were to slow campaigns marked by endless sieges, had never seen anything like that, and only at this point, alarmed by Charles VIII's successes, did they come to an agreement in order to rid the peninsula of the invaders. Fearing entrapment, the king of France prudently decided to return home after leaving a garrison in Naples, and, even if a battle at Fornovo ended without a clear victor (July 6, 1495), in the following months the Aragonese regained full control of their kingdom, expelling what remained of the French army.

The Italian system had bent without breaking. Charles VIII's expedition was not, however, without consequences, and not just because it exposed the palpable inequality between the small states of the peninsula and the great monarchies that had consolidated themselves elsewhere in Europe (a theme that Machiavelli would ceaselessly examine all his life). For example, Pisa, the most important Tuscan city under Florentine rule, took advantage of the upheaval to regain its independence and managed to defend it until 1509. The main regime change, however, occurred inside Florence, where Charles VIII's arrival in Tuscany led to the expulsion of the family that had governed it informally for three generations. The decisive clash had taken place exactly sixty years earlier, when the rich banker Cosimo de' Medici had defeated the opposing faction, led by the Albizzi and the Strozzi, thanks to a new coalition between families of ancient lineage and more recent prestige. At first, Cosimo's adversaries gained the upper hand, and in 1433 he had been condemned to exile; after a few months, however, a particularly favorable draw of electoral lots for his supporters had given the city a group of priors (the supreme magistrates, in office for just two months) who were determined to overturn the situation, and in 1434 it was the Albizzi and the Strozzi who had to leave Florence together with their allies. Upon his return home, Cosimo made sure that in the future chance would not play the same trick on him: he had his adversaries excluded from the bags containing the names of the citizens eligible for the offices so that they could not be drawn (in chapter 9 of *The Prince*, Machiavelli will speak of "fortunate cunning" for Cosimo's and his heirs' covert lordship). From that moment on, the Medici never officially repudiated the republican system, presenting themselves instead as the defenders of the commune's institutions, even if the real nature of their government was evident to all. As Enea Silvio Piccolomini, the future Pope Pius II, once replied to the bishop of Orte, Niccolò Palmieri, when the latter complained to him that "so beautiful a woman [Florence] was unjustly deprived of a husband [a prince]": "She lacks a husband, but not a lover [Cosimo]" (*Commentarii rerum memorabilium* 2.28). Inevitably, year after year, the Medici came to assert their power more explicitly, but especially after 1478, when the failed Pazzi conspiracy allowed them to further consolidate their control over the city; two years later, the institution of an oligarchic Council of Seventy served to tighten the traditional alliance with the principal families at a time when the descendants of Cosimo were clearly on the way to dispensing with any republican façade.

This discontinuity with respect to the past can be seen clearly in the Medicis' matrimonial policy. Cosimo and his son Piero married Florentine women from allied families, but Piero's son, Lorenzo the Magnificent, instead inaugurated a new strategy, which was aimed rather at rooting the Medici in the Italian aristocracy in order to lay the groundwork for their recognition as princes in their own right. Both Lorenzo and his son Piero thus married into the powerful Roman Orsini family, even if this choice risked irritating their Florentine supporters. The adroit Lorenzo always managed to calm any growing discontent, but when in 1492 he died suddenly at only forty-three, his son Piero proved to be less dexterous, inflaming tempers with a style of government more appropriate for a baronial clan like the Orsini than for a Florentine family, however wealthy and decorated.

In an already precarious situation caused by Charles VIII's arrival in Italy, Piero's indecision and the loss of Pisa precipitated the fall of the regime. The Medici were exiled and their properties incorporated by the state, and the commune's institutions were radically reformed. Florentine aristocrats looked with special favor at the Republic of Venice, which had a reputation for being well governed and experiencing enviable social stability. The political system of the so-called Serenissima was based on a complicated constitutional mechanism, according to which—alongside a doge elected for life (but entrusted with limited powers) and a large council made up of about three thousand citizens—it was a small senate composed of representatives from the major families that made all the important decisions. Why not imitate it? Perhaps, they suggested, in this way Florence could enjoy the same success.

In the end, however, the Florentines adopted a different solution, thanks in part to the intervention of a charismatic figure who enjoyed massive support in the city: the friar Girolamo Savonarola, a Dominican preacher originally from Ferrara, who in the months preceding Charles VIII's expedition had threatened terrible misfortunes had the citizens not repented of their sins, and hence he was believed to be endowed with prophetic powers. On his advice, the Florentines chose to refer all the important decisions to a Great Council of about 3,500 men, selected from the descendants of those who had occupied one of the major city offices in the last three generations and who were more than twenty-nine years old. (Machiavelli's household was not included because Niccolò's father had been conceived out of wedlock, and Florentine legislation rigorously discriminated against illegitimate children; one could even speculate whether the unpleasant discovery that both he and Bernardo were by birth a sort of second-rate citizen eventually contributed to Machiavelli's characteristic anticonformism and resistance to any kind of hierarchy inscribed in legal distinctions and family privilege.) Here was a radical change as well as an unparalleled experiment in popular participation in Europe in that period: for the first time, so many citizens were *directly* involved in the administration of the city. Out of a total population of about fifty thousand inhabitants (including women and children), about one adult male in three was admitted to the new governing body (in representation of around one thousand extended family units). Hence, by entrusting all the important decisions to such a large share of residents instead of to only a small senate, under Savonarola's guidance the new republican Florence greatly diverged from his initial model, Venice, which would remain the most respected example of closed aristocracy in Europe until its sudden fall in 1797.

Savonarola had presented himself as a peacemaker, but in fact he only further polarized Florentine politics with his controversial sermons, in which he called for a radical reform of the church's mores and threatened new ruin for those who did not follow his advice. The resultant clash with Alexander VI was so fierce that the pontiff excommunicated him and was ready to do the same to Florence, provoking the friar's overthrow. Savonarola was arrested, tried for heresy, and sentenced to be burned at the stake—a sudden collapse that will offer Machiavelli the inspiration for his pages in chapter 6 of *The Prince* on the "unarmed prophets," who are defeated because they lack the necessary strength to resist when their adversaries resort to violence against them.

With Savonarola's execution on May 23, 1498, the first—revolutionary—phase of the reborn republic came to a close. And from that moment on, Machiavelli would no longer limit himself to observing the political struggles from afar, as a crucial change in his own life was among the many consequences of the friar's downfall. First, however, we must take a step back in order to become acquainted with the future author of *The Prince* and the *Discourses on Livy*.

The Constant Reading of Ancient Things

Machiavelli is a son of humanism, even if a very peculiar one: a son who soon disavowed his own heritage but who, nevertheless, in his inexorable polemic against commonplaces, never stopped drawing on the teachings of his intellectual fathers—albeit in completely new forms. To put it more succinctly: Machiavelli shares with his humanist teachers the same readings but not their way of reading, and he almost always draws different, if not antithetical, lessons from them while still being engaged in (at least some of) their same problems. In all its constitutive ambivalence, such a conflicted relationship with the tradition in which he had been raised represents one of Machiavelli's most characteristic features and must always be kept in mind when discussing his works.

As we have seen, during Machiavelli's youth, humanism was one of the greatest sources of pride among the Italian elites, who considered themselves the only legitimate heirs of the Romans in the cultural field. No one did as much as Petrarch during the fourteenth century to advance the novel aesthetic values, not least through his efforts as an indefatigable correspondent with pontiffs, sovereigns, dukes, cardinals, and bishops throughout the continent; nevertheless, the origins of the movement were much older and dated back to the end of the thirteenth century, when a small group of poet-jurists from Padua began to approach Latin authors in ways that differed from the past. Throughout the Middle Ages, men of letters studied the vestiges of Roman antiquity in search of inspiration and cultural legitimacy without realizing precisely how far they were from their ancestors: for them it was as if they were still living in the same world. The Paduans Lovato Lovati and Albertino Mussato were the first to chart the historical distance in its full measure. By analyzing their favorite authors with unprecedented attention, it soon became clear to both of them that the ancients used a much richer and more complex Latin both at the lexical level and in their use of metrical and grammatical forms. Recognizing their own shortcomings in comparison with the great poets, orators, and historians of Rome, the first humanists worked to reconnect with what appeared to them to be a superior civilization and so to recover an elegance of diction that had been lost over the centuries.

Humanism was intertwined with the acute perception of a historical fracture in relation to the Roman past. At the same time, however, the humanists felt they could bridge the gap through the study of ancient style and language. Catching up with the Romans required devotion and scrupulous imitation, concentrating on previously overlooked grammatical details, but the result could also be very gratifying. Although this rediscovered Latin was much more difficult to understand for those who listened to it or read it without adequate preparation, it also sounded extraordinarily authoritative because suddenly those who were able to handle it properly seemed to express themselves as had the famous Scipio Africanus, say, or Julius Caesar. On the public stage, linguistic elegance could therefore translate into immediately tangible power.

This did not apply only to men of letters. The princes and the communal elites very soon embraced the new pedagogical curricula because, through invigorating contact with the classics, the humanists promised to make future rulers more virtuous—that is, worthier and more capable of administering public affairs in the interest of the whole community. It was the dream (so to speak) of a fully moralized politics through the assimilation of Greek and Latin masterworks. In an age of growing competition between different forms of government (especially in Italy, where republics, monarchies, great and small feudal lords, prince-bishops, the pope, and the emperor all coexisted in the same political space), the new education offered the ruling classes a formidable instrument of legitimization—one that was even more effective than dynastic succession and titles granted by the pope or the emperor. In a few decades the solid possession of classical culture was universally considered the best guarantee that those who had been enlightened by it at a young age would, once they grew up, fulfill their duties better than anyone else. For the humanists, it was as if their pupils were Romans who had risen from the dead.

Florence was associated with humanism at a very early stage (at least since the 1340s), but by the beginning of the fifteenth century the rediscovery of the study of Greek that spread from there made the Tuscan city the movement's undisputed head. After centuries in which nobody in the West had been able to read them, all the Greek texts that learned men of the time had only heard about from the great Latin writers had finally become accessible. Later, from the 1460s on, the invention of the printing press allowed for the circulation of all kinds of books in thousands and thousands of copies, including the newly revived classics. But although other centers, first and foremost Naples and Rome, soon started promoting the original humanist literature that was nurtured by the study of ancient authors, Florence maintained its position of primacy.

In 1469, to be born in Florence meant being brought to life in a special city, but Machiavelli's education must also have been influenced by his family background. His father Bernardo graduated in law and, from what we know, was a man of solid reading, well versed in the classics and curious about new books, or so his small personal library indicates (even if, being illegitimate, Bernardo was never admitted to the Guild of Judges and Notaries and therefore could never practice the profession). A few hexameters written by him survive in manuscript form, and although they hardly show a strong poetic vocation, they confirm his proximity to humanistic culture, as does the fact that among Bernardo's friends was a famous man of letters: no one less than the chancellor of the Republic of Florence, Bartolomeo Scala, who introduced Niccolò's father as the other main character in a dialogue on the essence of laws (*De legibus et iudiciis*, composed in 1483). In one of his fables (collected in *Centum apologi*, 1481), Scala presented a noble young man of illegitimate birth who blames the laws that deprived him not only of a conspicuous inheritance but also of the honors that came from a full belonging to his homeland; one could wonder if, in echoing such a bitter complaint, Scala was thinking also of his friend Bernardo's exclusion from civic life.

Unfortunately, very little can be said with confidence about Machiavelli's education, but what we do know is very important for bringing into focus the originality of his later works. In the archives there is no trace, for example, of his enrollment in a university, even if it seems that at some point he benefited from the guidance of Marcello Virgilio Adriani, a respected philologist, professor of poetics and rhetoric at the University of Florence since 1494, and Scala's successor as the head of the Florentine chancery since February 1498. However it was achieved, the high quality of Machiavelli's education is beyond dispute. Although he probably never learned Greek and wrote almost exclusively in Italian, his works exhibit a deep intimacy with a large number of classical texts, including several authors only recently rediscovered thanks to the Latin translations made by the humanists, such as the Greek historians Dionysius of Halicarnassus (printed in 1480), Thucydides (1483), and Herodian (1493) and the military theorist Aelian the Tactician (1487).

Further evidence of Machiavelli's humanistic training can be found in a manuscript now preserved in the Vatican Library in Rome. At an unspecified time in the 1490s, Machiavelli transcribed the *Eunuchus*, a comedy by the second-century-BCE Roman playwright Terence, and the *De rerum natura*, by the first-century-BCE Roman poet-philosopher Lucretius—possibly with a view to a philologically improved print edition that never came to light. If, in the first case, we are not dealing with a particularly unusual choice, since Terence was an author frequently deployed in the classroom (schoolchildren sometimes even staged his works in Latin), Machiavelli's interest in Lucretius appears much more significant. The *De rerum natura* (discovered by the humanist Poggio Bracciolini in 1417 in a German monastery and printed for the first time in 1473) contained a poetic exposition of Epicurus's controversial philosophy, which throughout the Middle Ages had attracted the ire of the church. Lucretius identified happiness with pleasure (which amounted to the absence of pain), affirmed free will and the power of chance, proclaimed that all material substances of the universe were composed of atoms, praised the techniques that helped primitive men emerge from the original condition of need, argued for the mortality of the soul (inviting his readers not to fear death), and proclaimed the disinterest of the gods in human affairs—all positions that were in open conflict not just with religious orthodoxy but also with Renaissance science (which in its fundamental elements still depended on Aristotle and his commentators). In short, the fact that the young and already nonconformist Machiavelli was intrigued by the *De rerum natura* to the point of taking on the onerous task of transcribing it is not a minor biographical anecdote.

Machiavelli's first experiments in vernacular translation probably date back to this period, as is evidenced by a still unpolished Italian version of Terence's *Andria* (which he then entirely reworked, with greater skill, in his later years). Even in this case, translating classical theater was far from an obvious choice. At that time ancient comedies and tragedies were still represented exclusively in Latin (or even in Greek, as in the case of Sophocles's *Electra*, performed with great success by Scala's daughter Alessandra in 1493), and only a few years earlier, in 1486, the staging at the court of Ferrara of the third-century-BCE Roman playwright Plautus's *Menaechmi* had inaugurated a series of productions in the vernacular that, again in Ferrara, would culminate in the representation of the first comedy composed according to Latin models in any modern language: the *Cassaria* by Ludovico Ariosto (1508). That means that the young Machiavelli promptly tried to follow the experiments that were being carried out on the other side of the Apennines, in the city that headed the attempts to derive the secret formula for laughter from the classics.

Machiavelli was not destined to go down this road even though his passion for the theater and his loyalty to Terence would bear extraordinary fruit in his mature years, when his comedies would be successfully performed in Florence, Rome, and Venice. His early experiments from the 1490s, however, shed light on the particular character of his love for the classics. Rather than engaging in the stringent philological study of Roman and Greek texts and fragments to which most of the humanists dedicated their efforts (and in which Adriani excelled), Machiavelli was interested in *reviving* the masterpieces of the past by making them accessible to a broader public and bringing them back onto the stage. This was what Adriani's pupil tried to achieve with his version of the *Andria*. In different ways, however, it is also what he would try to do with ancient historians and military theorists later in his life, when he attempted to extract from his favorite books Rome's practical wisdom, which his teachers, with their emphasis on the texts' linguistic and scholarly aspects, neither sought nor had been able to grasp. It was necessary to take another road. And Machiavelli at that point would no longer hesitate to commit the inevitable parricide.

The Sustained Experience of Modern Things

On June 19, 1498, the Great Council chose Ser Niccolò Machiavelli, son of Bernardo, a twenty-nine-year-old humanist of great promise, for the coveted position of second chancellor of the republic. While it was up to the first chancellor to keep alive the tradition that had brought prestige to Florence, when eminent humanists such as Coluccio Salutati, Leonardo Bruni, and Poggio Bracciolini had managed the official correspondence with popes, emperors, and kings in their elegant Latin, the appointee to this less prestigious (but more hands-on) office was responsible for the letters sent in the vernacular in the *distretto* (that is, in Florence's more recently acquired territories, like Arezzo, Pistoia, Montepulciano, and Cortona). It is possible that his father's friendship with Scala and his personal relationship with Adriani (then the first chancellor in office) contributed to Machiavelli's appointment to such an important position. His aversion to Savonarola might have counted in his favor more than anything else, however, given that when Machiavelli entered the chancery, the ashes of the stake where the friar was burned were still warm and the official he was called upon to succeed was a well-known supporter of Savonarola. In such a pugnacious context Adriani's pupil must have seemed a bulwark against a return to the past in a Florence where the preacher's followers, the so-called Piagnoni, were (and would long remain) quite numerous.

Service in the chancery was to become a sort of second education for Machiavelli. As he wrote in the dedication letter of *The Prince*, from those years he had gained "sustained experience of modern things" very different from the "continuous reading about ancient ones" that had engaged him during his training as a humanist. A secretary of the second chancery carried out the most varied tasks, some of which were quite humble. For example, besides writing thousands of letters on negligible administrative matters, for some time Machiavelli drafted the minutes of the *pratiche*, the informal meetings where the magistrates and the most eminent citizens prepared the sessions of the Great Council by drawing up an agenda and deciding which measures and which candidates to bring up for a vote. But the importance of the position lay not so much (or only) in what Machiavelli did but in where he was. At a time when all public offices in Florence were of very short duration (generally two to four months), the officials of the chancery were among the few who enjoyed a close and continuous view of the republic's policies (the other exception being members of the leading families, who were consulted on all major issues because of their recognized political experience). A constant flow of news connected the Palazzo della Signoria with the whole of Europe (rumors, official dispatches, letters in code, confidences), and there was no information of importance to which the secretary did not have access. Above all, it was there that the republic's moves were planned and countermeasures were taken, at a time when Florence's very survival was threatened by the exiled Medici and, more generally, by Italy's instability. However informally, a chancellor respected for his political acumen was called upon to offer his counsel on the most diverse issues, often influencing the choices that were then made in the appropriate institutional venues.

Precisely because he was an expert on the political landscape of Italy and beyond, the chancellor was also a perfect candidate for the most delicate diplomatic missions (although Machiavelli's predecessors had rarely performed this task). In this capacity, between 1499 and 1512 Machiavelli carried out twenty-six legations to minor figures of Italian politics but also kings, popes, and emperors in France, Switzerland, and the southern provinces of the Holy Roman Empire: to sound out their intentions, negotiate agreements, make alliances, and obtain and grant aid. At the same time, during his journeys in each of these countries Machiavelli became familiar with unusual habits, traditions, and practices, and this firsthand knowledge of the world significantly contributed to his openness of mind. Simply put, traveling across Europe accustomed him to diversity and helped him throw off the entrenched prejudices of his time. It was therefore probably also because of this curiosity and tolerance toward cultural differences that, even when Machiavelli analyzes extra-European powers like the Ottoman Empire, he always avoids ethnic stereotypes and judges the states' successes and failures exclusively on political criteria (instead of on their religious affiliation, as was customary among his contemporaries).

It is no coincidence that Machiavelli's most prestigious missions took place after 1502. That year, in fact, marked the most important phase of institutional discontinuity in Florence since 1494. For some time the most powerful families and the common citizens who were gathered in the Great Council had struggled to reach an agreement on widely varying issues: from the prosecution of the war for Pisa and the revenue system (with the aristocrats endorsing a flat tax, while the people was in favor of progressive taxation) to how magistrates should be chosen (the aristocrats championed elections, which—a little counterintuitively—benefited them, but in 1499 the Great Council opted instead for designation by lot among the citizens who had received the most votes). At the height of the conflict, the "mighty" (*grandi*) even refused to underwrite new loans with the commune, threatening to leave the republic without the money to pay for an army, and they began to withdraw from the magistracies to the point of paralyzing the city's government. Such maneuvers (quite unusual in their harshness) were designed to put pressure on the Great Council to reform the constitution, which—in the aristocrats' hopes—would have led to the creation of a senate of two hundred members (elected for life), where all the most important issues would be decided, more or less as was the case in Venice. In the end, however, the partisans of the "broad government" (popular rule) and those of the "narrow government" (oligarchic rule) agreed instead on the institution of a "standardbearer of justice" for life, on the model of the Venetian doge, in order to ensure above all a greater continuity in Florentine foreign policy. The choice fell on one of the city's most respected figures, Piero Soderini, a member of a family that had supported the Medici until 1494 but had then sided with the new republican rule. Given his origins, the aristocrats saw in him an ideal instrument for carrying out their plans and introducing an all-powerful senate, but, to their great surprise and disappointment, Soderini, once elected, pursued the opposite agenda, soon becoming a champion of the people and finding in Machiavelli a man he could trust in the administration.

It is impossible to say which of Soderini's choices were influenced by Machiavelli in the following ten years. In at least one case, however, his contribution seems beyond question. In the fifteenth century, humanists had often lashed out against mercenary troops, calling for a return to the conscription of citizens in imitation of the ancients (and also of the Florentines themselves, until 1351), but in Florence the inutility of hired condottieri had become clear to everybody during the siege of Pisa. To resolve the situation, Machiavelli persuaded Soderini to undertake an audacious reform. During Charles VIII's expedition, the Italians had discovered the effectiveness of the Swiss infantry, which was armed with six-meter-long pikes and organized in squares of hundreds and sometimes thousands of men, capable not only of stopping heavy cavalry but also of attacking and routing their enemies. To operate well, soldiers equipped with such pikes did not need to excel in the use of weapons as long as they knew how to move in unison with absolute precision, but once they slipped out of formation, they became vulnerable to counterattacks. And since these elaborate movements were easier to learn than the techniques of individual combat, in 1504 Machiavelli convinced the standardbearer to have the trusted (noncitizen) inhabitants of the *contado* (the countryside closer to Florence) trained in these new military skills.

Through Machiavelli's plan, Florence would soon find itself able to face much more powerful adversaries by fielding a faithful and proficient army. The new style of warfare introduced by Charles VIII (centrality of the infantry, emphasis on battles in the open field instead of sieges, a high speed of action, and especially the unprecedented magnitude of the war contingents) made such a response urgent. Hence, despite the aristocrats' opposition, the first parade of troops in 1506 was a grand public event and one that was talked about all over Italy. Venice immediately imitated Florence, and when Pisa was finally reconquered in 1509, many credited the success to the new militia and its promoter Machiavelli.

At the same time, the reform potentially had other positive effects. The militia would have given the standardbearer an extraordinary means of exerting pressure on his internal adversaries at a time when the city's oligarchy, disappointed by his pro-popular attitude, had begun to oppose Soderini openly (some judged his military reform such an impending menace that the aristocratic leader and learned humanist Bernardo Rucellai, fearing a coup, decided to quit the city for some time). But even without going to such extremes, Machiavelli's innovation would have damaged the most powerful families in other ways. In order to hire mercenaries, the republic was accustomed to granting very high interest rates (14 percent) to the wealthiest Florentines, who provided the money needed for the war and, by doing so, profited from their city's difficulties (just to make a quick comparison, in the same years agriculture did not grant more than 5 percent, whereas a riskier investment in a commercial company could earn the lender an 8 percent profit). At a time when nearly the entire budget of the republic went to subsidizing the siege of Pisa, the militia would have allowed Florence to free itself from the public debt that strangled the city's finances and, at the same time, remove an important source of income for those who speculated on the war. Stronger on the battlefield, Florence would no longer be blackmailable by the oligarchy.

In his later works Machiavelli would devote considerable space to military problems, but such incessant attention is not surprising when we consider how much energy he had spent on his militia project during his chancery years. A further result of that prolonged experience was that Machiavelli would never forget that war is not just a question of military force. Even before a single battle is fought, armies move huge sums of money, as was especially evident in Renaissance Italy, from the major states, forced to enlist mercenary troops for their defense, to the condottieri princes eager to put themselves at the service of the highest bidder (with a dangerous disequilibrium in the trade balance for the employers), but also from the ordinary citizens (who were obliged to pay substantial interest on public debt through taxes) to the richest families (who held that public debt).

At the same time, depending on the combat techniques that were adopted, war also determined the relative political weight of the different social classes. Machiavelli's generation was the first in Italy to witness the decline of the heavy cavalry, which had dominated warfare throughout the Middle Ages, and the rise of the infantry of pikemen, which gave common people a power that had not been available to them since antiquity. Roman history taught that the plebs had managed to obtain considerable concessions from the patricians precisely by threatening to withdraw their support in war (an aspect that Machiavelli would later discuss in depth in his *Discourses on Livy*). Following this historical lesson, a militarized Florence would therefore inevitably have been more favorable to the people, and it is exactly in this direction that, step by step, Machiavelli wanted to lead his city, a project that immediately won him the hatred of a considerable part of the oligarchy, which, in retaliation, tried to have Machiavelli excluded from ambassadorships with the excuse of his father's illegitimate birth.

In those years, Pisa was not Florence's only concern. The political situation remained fluid, and while the republic was engaged in recovering its principal outlet to the sea, it also had to keep its eye on new threats. In the mayhem of the Italian wars Machiavelli rapidly learned that a condition of permanent uncertainty and lethal competition inevitably characterizes foreign affairs; as he would eventually write to his friend Francesco Guicciardini, turning back to his youth: "Always, as far back as I can remember, war has either been going on or has been talked about" (January 3, 1526). In 1498 Charles VIII's death and Louis XII's succession to the throne inaugurated a new phase of instability. The events of 1494 had shown how vulnerable Italy was, and the new French king immediately set his sights on Lombardy, boasting of his distant kinship with the extinct Visconti dynasty. The duke of Milan, Ludovico Sforza, who had been the main architect of Charles VIII's expedition, was quickly overwhelmed. Not satisfied with this easy victory, Louis XII decided to resume his predecessor's plans for the conquest of Naples, but this time he decided to take precautions by signing a secret agreement through which the Neapolitan Kingdom would be divided with the other major European power, the Spain of Ferdinand and Isabella. In this case, too, all resistance proved to be useless, and the Italian branch of the Aragonese house was soon forced into exile. Thus, in less than two years, between September 1499 and August 1501, two of the five regional powers on which the Italian system had relied for decades were annihilated, a development that completely dissolved what remained of fifteenth-century balance. Nevertheless, Louis XII did not succeed in his projects, for he soon came into conflict with Ferdinand, and, after an irrecoverable defeat at the battle of Garigliano (December 29, 1503), he had to forfeit all his rights over Naples.

As for Florence (in these years allied with France), the main menace came from the hyperactivity of two impetuous pontiffs, who would both repeatedly materialize in Machiavelli's writings over the following years: Alexander VI Borgia (pope from 1492 to 1503) and Julius II della Rovere (pope from 1503 to 1513). Spanish by birth and the nephew of another pontiff (Callixtus III Borgia), Alexander VI dedicated most of his energies to ensuring his descendants a territorial state in central Italy, and he came to symbolize the corruption of the Renaissance papacy—even in today's popular imagination. To carry out his plan, he went along with the designs of his son Cesare, who, by exploiting military and financial support from his father, quickly succeeded in founding a powerful duchy in the lands formally subject to the church, between Emilia-Romagna, the Marches, and Umbria. The Florentines were very concerned about what looked like a slow encirclement, and in an attempt to come to an agreement with the Borgias, they often sent Machiavelli on missions to Cesare (who would later provide him with a model of political wisdom in *The Prince*). In the end, however, upon Alexander VI's death, the Borgia state rapidly dissolved, and Florence unexpectedly found itself free of a major threat. Everyone in Italy felt relieved. Hence, a famous Neapolitan poet, Iacopo Sannazaro, perfidiously commented on Cesare's meteoric rise and fall in a couple of Latin epigrams: "Borgia wishes as his motto: 'Either nothing or Caesar.' Why not, / since he can be at once Cesare and nothing?" and "You were conquering everything, you were hoping for everything, Cesare. / Everything is passing away. You begin to be nothing."

Julius II, like Alexander the nephew of a pope (in his case the bellicose Sixtus IV della Rovere), pursued a policy different from his predecessor's, but his designs proved even more dangerous to Florence. Unlike Alexander VI, Julius II was not a nepotistic pontiff committed to favoring his own family but rather worked hard to recover the territories that only nominally obeyed the church—even if this meant engaging in an almost uninterrupted sequence of wars. In 1506 the pope brought Perugia and Bologna back to obedience; in 1508 he organized a general alliance against Venice (the League of Cambrai), intending to reclaim the territories in Romagna that had been occupied by the Serenissima after Borgia's downfall; he had Venice crushed at Agnadello (May 14, 1509), permanently derailing its plans for expansion in the mainland; finally, in 1511, he raised another international coalition (the Holy League) to oust France from Italy.

The main victim of this last move was Florence. The opposing French and Spanish-Papal coalitions clashed near Ravenna (April 11, 1512), and while France got the better on the battlefield, the death in combat of the French general Gaston de Foix eventually resulted in the loss of the Duchy of Milan for Louis XII. Florence, which was still allied to France, suddenly found itself isolated. The unthinkable had happened, and from that moment on the situation deteriorated ever more quickly. The Spanish army marched on Tuscany, sacking the city of Prato (August 29), only twenty kilometers from Florence. At that point, exploiting the terror that the news of Prato unleashed in the city, some armed aristocrats forced Soderini, under the threat of death, to flee into exile (August 31), and they opened the gates to the Spaniards, who in turn brought back the Medici (September 1) and coerced the Florentine people to vote for the abrogation of the 1494 institutions (September 16). It was a real coup: rather than sharing power with ordinary citizens in the Great Council, the oligarchy (or at least a conspicuous part of it) had preferred that Cosimo's descendants rule the city again. Two months later, on November 7, Machiavelli was dismissed from his post after fourteen years of service, and he moved to his country estate in Sant'Andrea in Percussina, some twenty kilometers south of Florence (where, on clear days, he nonetheless had a direct view of the city's cathedral dome).

2

The People's Prince

Yesterday Cardinal [Giulio] de' Medici asked me hastily if I knew that you hired Niccolò Machiavelli. And, when I answered that I did not know nor believed this, he told me these formal words: "I do not believe it either; however, as it has been so reported to us from Florence, I remind Giuliano that this is neither his need nor ours. . . . Write him that I urge him not to mingle with Niccolò."

—Pietro Ardinghelli [Leo X's secretary] to
Giuliano de' Medici, February 14, 1515

Illusion, Foundations, and Flux

The Princessa: Machiavelli for Women; The Mafia Manager: A Guide to Corporate Machiavelli; Machiavelli in Brussels: The Art of Lobbying the EU (a best-seller with a sequel: *More Machiavelli in Brussels*); *The Machiavellian's Guide to Womanizing* (by Nick Casanova); *Machiavelli for Moms: Maxims on the Effective Governance of Children; The Machiavellian Librarian: Winning Allies, Combating Budget Cuts, and Influencing Stakeholders* . . . Machiavelli's most famous work continues to fuel a lively stream of imitations (somewhere between a self-help manual and a treatise on leadership), inspired by his reputation as a cynical adviser of moral turpitude. Clearly, the 1513 treatise has little to do with such gross counterfeits and misinterpretations. Nevertheless, volumes like these can also teach us something precious about the real *Prince*.

Why this success, then? Beyond the popularity of the brand (one relaunched in recent years by television series like *Borgia*, 2011–2014, and video games like *Assassin's Creed II*, 2009–2010), it is important to recognize that there is something in Machiavelli that never ceases to captivate. With its extreme frankness about power relationships, *The Prince* not only reveals something previously unheard about the true (nasty?) nature of politics but also conveys a general vision of the world that largely transcends the book's specific examples and wins the attention of today's readers even when it discusses issues and historical events quite remote from our present. The appeal of *The Prince*'s lessons depends therefore first and foremost on their (presumed) immediate applicability to a great number of different situations (for example, the Italian nineteenth-century poet and philosopher Giacomo Leopardi spoke of a "High Life Machiavellianism" in regard to cynical everyday uses of *The Prince*'s precepts in salon society, resulting in a constant war of all against all).

One of the fundamental elements of Machiavelli's world is the puzzling rift between what is and what appears to be—the universal domain of illusion, from which only a few wise people are able to escape. *The Prince* does nothing but repeat this mantra: things are not as they seem, and everyone deceives, but, moreover, everyone is ready to be deceived. Even rulers are no exception to this widespread blindness, as is evidenced by the willingness of Renaissance lords to pay substantial sums for an official title from the pope or emperor, believing that real power depends on words and labels. The shrewd politician, on the other hand, is one who correctly estimates the forces in the field: his gaze is far-reaching, seeing beyond the immediate consequences of every action, but it is also penetrating, because, while ordinary people linger at the surface, he gets down to the core of things. And, if in *The Prince* this invitation to focus on the essentials means putting military capacity and the support of the people before everything else, the invitation not to trust appearances and to discern what is really relevant in a given situation has much broader implications and remains valid centuries later—including in a world where feudal titles no longer exist and political struggles only occasionally evolve into armed clashes.

The other characteristic feature of Machiavelli's universe is the constant mobility of all things—the recognition that people and states are being dragged along in an unstoppable flow that disorients and confuses but above all risks overwhelming the unprepared. The judicious politician understands the power of unforeseen events and organizes his defenses ahead of time, evaluating his future ability to resist: he worries about the "foundation," to use an image very dear to Machiavelli that refers to what is rooted in the earth and allows the entire edifice to last no matter what happens, in opposition to the perennial instability of fortune that Renaissance authors instead associated with water. The prince must therefore behave first and foremost like an engineer who promptly raises the appropriate embankments against the coming storms (chapter 25).

However, instability can also be used to one's advantage. Once defenses are in place, one must learn how to move effectively in such a dangerous world of false appearances and reflections. Whereas ancient and humanistic political thought praised the Stoic and then Christian virtue of fortitude, thanks to which men remain faithful to their principles in any given situation, Machiavelli instead commends the capacity to adjust. It is a decisive shift, even if also in doing this he implicitly refers to another classical tradition: that of rhetorical treatises by Aristotle, Cicero, and the first-century Roman orator Quintilian, where the key to success lies in the speaker's ability to adapt his words according to time, place, audience, and circumstances in order to win the approval of his public. Machiavelli moves in their footsteps, and this is why one of the most memorable figures in *The Prince* is the centaur Chiron, who (very differently from the humanists' ideal rulers, completely defenseless as they are when arms speak and diplomacy is silent) can fight equally well with both human and beastly weapons—in the latter instance knowing how to conceal the lion's violence thanks to the fox's cunning (chapter 18). Like a surfer or skier, who keeps his balance by shifting his weight here and there to make the most of the kinetic energy of the wave or slope, Machiavelli's prince will focus on his dexterity and promptness of reaction to prevail over enemies, modifying his posture as soon as external conditions evolve, thereby winning stability in a dynamic context.

As long as one masters change, the general context of instability is not necessarily a bad thing. In fact, constant transformation brings many opportunities to those who know how to conform to "the actual truth of the thing" (chapter 15), having taken precautions against surprises and learned to adapt to any vicissitude. Only a few people, of course, are able to do so—but it is precisely this much-valued insight that Machiavelli intends to share with his disciples. Even those who know nothing about the context in which *The Prince* was written and are uneasy with its numerous historical references immediately sense just how high the stakes of his teaching are. Politics is a very difficult art, but—Machiavelli pledges—it is an art that can be learned and absorbed without necessarily requiring years and years of study and assimilation of the classics, as the humanists believed. With Machiavelli as instructor, even the arcana of power suddenly seem within everyone's reach. True or false, *The Prince*'s success depends today above all on this promise and on the peculiar euphoria that its pages still transmit. The future is open: any goal can be achieved. And, five hundred years after Machiavelli's death, readers are guided by such an aspiration to put their trust in his teachings.

The Prince as a "Mirror"

When, in September 1512, the sudden return of the Medici ended Machiavelli's career, he was, by the standards of the day, an aged man. In Florence, at that time, people of forty changed their lifestyle: they tried to eat very little meat and to abstain from sex because they knew that death was imminent and hoped that sacrifices on earth would translate into a smoother journey in the afterlife and a shorter stay in Purgatory. Being forty-three thus made the loss of his position in the chancery especially difficult for Machiavelli—but things got even worse over the following months. On February 18, 1513, a plot to kill the Medici family's leading figures was discovered, and Machiavelli's name was found on a list of citizens whom the conspirators Pietro Paolo Boscoli and Agostino Capponi had schemed to involve in their plan; for this reason, as a precautionary measure, Machiavelli was imprisoned and subjected to torture to induce him to confess. In this situation people often admit crimes that they have not committed just to put an end to their suffering, but Machiavelli kept silent, and, while he was awaiting his release from jail, he received sensational news: on March 9, the conclave had elected as the new pope Cardinal Giovanni de' Medici (son of Lorenzo the Magnificent and brother of Piero), who had taken the name of Leo X. He was the first Florentine in history to ascend to the papal throne.

Machiavelli had escaped death, but his problems were not entirely resolved. What prospects did he have? Not wealthy enough to retire to his country home and determined not to participate in any conspiratorial activity, the former secretary of the republic had but two alternatives. He could go into exile, perhaps seeking a position elsewhere as secretary (and in fact, in the following years, he received job offers from the republic of Ragusa, present-day Dubrovnik, in Dalmatia, and from the Medici condottiere Giovanni dalle Bande Nere). Or he could, instead, try to get back into Florence's political game, drawing on previous connections to persuade the informal lords of his city to put an end to the interdict that weighed on him for his friendship with Soderini.

Machiavelli chose the second path, and in the spring of 1513 he began to sound out by letter one of the aristocrats closest to the Medici, Francesco Vettori, then Florentine ambassador to

Rome, with whom Machiavelli had shared a long and difficult diplomatic mission to Emperor Maximilian I five years before. As Machiavelli wrote to him: "Fortune has made that, since I do not know how to talk about either the Silk and the Wool Guild, or about profits and losses, I have to talk about politics—and I need either to take a vow of silence or to discuss this" (April 19). In the uncertainty of the moment, however, everyone had to be very careful, and, despite the polite pressure applied by Machiavelli (who, in his letters, interspersed his jokes with acute analyses of the international situation in the hope that Vettori would show them to the pontiff), his friend did not want to, or simply could not, help him.

Machiavelli was faced with this latest setback when in the summer of 1513 the Florentine militia was suspended and the pope entrusted informal government of the city to his nephew Lorenzo (in place of his brother Giuliano, who until then had managed the family affairs in Florence). At this point Machiavelli decided it was time to act, even without Vettori's assistance: he would go directly to Lorenzo. From 1494 to 1512 the Medici had survived in exile mainly thanks to three assets—the ties by marriage to the powerful Orsini clan, the support in the Papal Curia of Giovanni (who in 1489 had been appointed cardinal at age thirteen in exchange for a large sum illegally grabbed by his father from Florence's public finances), and their enormous family wealth, prudently hidden by Lorenzo the Magnificent through a network of accommodating front men in the event of political catastrophe—but nobody knew exactly how they would behave once they returned to Florence. It was therefore necessary to proceed with extreme caution, and here the social conventions of the time left only one option to Machiavelli. While only the *pareri*, the "counsels" that were explicitly requested or came from a trusted friend, had any hope of being taken into consideration (a rule as valid today as it was in sixteenth-century Italy), it was not unusual for Renaissance men of letters to seek the protection of rulers by offering them the fruit of their imagination or their studies—poems, collections of sonnets, novellas, or tracts on the most diverse subjects. Obtaining a reward for such gifts was not a foregone conclusion, but nothing precluded Machiavelli from pursuing this path. According to an unwritten code, once the dedicatee had received the book, he could either accept the present (and was then obliged to show his appreciation in a variety of ways, and not just in pecuniary terms) or refuse it (thus avoiding the obligation of gratitude). For Machiavelli, who in *The Prince*'s dedicatory letter explicitly mentions his past experiences and his desire to work for Lorenzo, an eventual sign of approval from the young Medici could have reopened the doors to politics, in the chancery or elsewhere.

Of all the literary genres practiced by humanists, Machiavelli obviously chose the one that best suited his skills and the situation of Lorenzo, who had returned to Florence from a long exile at the age of twenty-one without any previous experience in government. The short pamphlet composed in late 1513 is thus what his contemporaries would have called a *speculum principis*, a "mirror for the prince": a treatise on the virtues of the ruler and the administration of the state. The image derives from the first-century treatise *De clementia*, where the Roman philosopher Seneca used it to suggest to his pupil and addressee—the young emperor Nero—that he could easily recognize himself in the portrait of the ideal ruler that his teacher was sending to him. Since *De clementia* and other major ancient "mirrors for princes" (such as the fourth-century-BCE Xenophon's *Cyropaedia* and Isocrates's *To Nicocles*, both repeatedly translated from Greek into Latin) enjoyed enormous success during the Renaissance and were widely imitated by the humanists (like Petrarch in his letters; Giovanni Pontano in his *De principe*, 1465, printed in 1490; and Francesco Patrizi, among many others), it is hardly surprising that Machiavelli decided to address one of them to Lorenzo.

The *speculum* genre's recent blossoming was undoubtedly linked to the centrality of pedagogy in the humanists' political vision. Machiavelli, too, shows an obvious dependence on this tradition, from which he draws several themes, such as the list of qualities necessary for the government of the state (chapter 15), the danger of hatred (chapters 16–17 and 19), the opposition between love and fear (chapter 17), the usefulness of secretaries (chapters 22–23), and the power of virtue over fortune in human life (chapter 25). At the same time, with a quick look any Renaissance reader would have noted a conspicuous absence. All fifteenth-century *specula* are characterized by large pedagogical sections that, in the case of the most scrupulous authors (such as Patrizi in his *De institutione reipublicae*, 1471, and *De regno*, 1484), could occupy dozens (if not hundreds) of pages on topics ranging from architecture to rhetoric, from literature to philosophy, from astronomy to astrology, from mathematics to music: proof that the humanists' good princes had to compete with their teachers in terms of knowledge in order to properly exercise the difficult task for which they were destined at birth. On the contrary, apart from a quick reference in chapter 14 to the importance of historical knowledge and the benefits of hunting in preparation for war (a topic that would be eventually discussed also in *Discourses* 3.39), no such didactic concern appears in *The Prince*.

Quite simply, Machiavelli is not interested in such matters, because he rejects the humanists' faith that classical culture makes rulers more virtuous and temperate. Lorenzo had studied both Latin and Greek for many years (as was customary for the sons of good families), but—*The Prince* insinuates—this is not what he will need in order to govern Florence. Hence Machiavelli intends to guide the young Medici in a completely different direction, breaking clamorously with the intellectual tradition in which he had been educated. As chapter 14 boldly declares: "A prince should therefore have no other objective, nor any other thought, nor take anything for his own art save warfare and its ordering and discipline, because that is the only art expected of those who command." Machiavelli's fracture with humanism will depend first and foremost on this rebuttal of fifteenth-century political pedagogy.

The Prince as a "Counsel"

For all its brevity, *The Prince* is a book of many layers and one that does several different things at once. It is, as we have seen, a gift designed to open a channel of communication with Florence's new lords. And, at the same time, it is Machiavelli's résumé, as the many references to his past experience in the chancery suggest (for instance his various meetings with Cesare Borgia, Louis XII, Emperor Maximilian I, Julius II, and their counselors). Yet *The Prince* is so much more—and under the pretext of paying homage to Lorenzo, it offers him a written "counsel" not too different from those that for ten years Machiavelli had dispensed orally to Soderini.

Such an ambition implies a very peculiar rhetorical strategy. Predictably enough, in the dedication letter Machiavelli carefully respects all the conventions and shows himself obsequious to Lorenzo, but as soon as the treatise begins, a reader familiar with similar works is immediately struck by his extreme outspokenness. While traditional "mirrors" always confirm to the dedicatee that he already possesses everything he needs to govern, Machiavelli tells Lorenzo exactly the opposite: even if the Medici are at the height of their fortune, their position remains precarious; their strength depends entirely on the pope, and popes, it is known, on average do not rule for more than ten years; as soon as Leo X is no longer protecting them, the status of his family may prove too fragile to withstand the upheavals that always accompany the end of a pontificate (as illustrated in chapter 7 of *The Prince* by the fall of even the brave and skilled Cesare Borgia). That, at least, is what a man like Machiavelli—who knew how to look beyond the glittering surface—saw.

It is unlikely that anyone had ever spoken in such terms to the pope's nephew before. But Machiavelli had no choice but to adopt this tone because Lorenzo would only accept the suggestions in *The Prince* if he recognized the precariousness of his own position. Thus, Machiavelli proceeds exactly as an expert advertiser would: he knows that in order to sell his product (in this case, his militia), it is necessary first to instill in the potential buyer a sense of insecurity—and then of need. Once Lorenzo has been persuaded that mercenary and allied troops are useless (as asserted especially in chapters 12–13), that he lacks something essential, and that only Machiavelli can provide it, the rest will follow easily.

Of the many elements that make *The Prince* unique within its genre, one of the most striking is the final chapter, in which Machiavelli assigns Lorenzo a great mission that will assure him eternal glory: to free Italy from foreign invaders. Several medieval and humanistic "mirrors" had been composed for a new sovereign's succession, but in *none of them* had the author ever tried to influence his dedicatee's political strategies, not even in the vaguest or most general terms, apart from telling him to continue on the path of virtue. Machiavelli, on the contrary, has a precise plan for Lorenzo, and this element alone would be enough to render *The Prince* different from all the (apparently similar) treatises that preceded it.

No less daring are the contents of the "counsel." Reduced to its essentials, Machiavelli's advice can be summarized in four points: (1) the Florentine aristocrats and the Spaniards have brought the Medici back to power, but neither is a reliable "foundation" without one's own army and popular support; (2) only through Machiavelli's reforms will Florence be able to equip itself with an adequate military, but first Lorenzo must strengthen his grip on the oligarchy, which has always wholly resisted this project; (3) a prince can arm his subjects only if he is liked by them, and for this reason, once the militia is reintroduced, Lorenzo will have to cultivate the support of the common citizens and not of the "mighty"; and (4) only at that point will Lorenzo finally be able to devote himself to what all "new princes" must do to strengthen their position: launch a great enterprise, which in 1513 could only be the liberation of Italy from the last foreign power remaining on the peninsula, the Spaniards.

Undermine the oligarchy and oust Ferdinand of Aragon: it is difficult to imagine a more complete reversal of alliances, and such a plan has much to say about the man who conceived it. If Machiavelli had simply been a cynic, willing to do anything to regain his position (the grounds on which so many have reproached him), it would have been enough for him to send a traditional "mirror" to Lorenzo as a sign of his willingness to serve the new order. *The Prince*, on the contrary, pursues a much more ambitious objective: to persuade the Medici to reorganize the militia. For such a task, it is obvious, no one would have been as qualified as Machiavelli; in this case, however, a hypothetical agreement with the Medici would have been made on his terms, and not theirs, with Lorenzo called to take Soderini's place in sponsoring Machiavelli's old project. Somehow, at the end of the day, Lorenzo ought to have become the people's prince.

In politics you cannot choose your friends—but you can choose your enemies, and Machiavelli's principal opponents always were (and remained after the fall of the republic) the Florentine "mighty." Trying to convince Lorenzo to break the alliance with the aristocrats who had orchestrated the coup against Soderini was obviously a long shot and maybe even a dangerous proposition, but Machiavelli was probably inclined to risk it not least because of his (correct) supposition that the young Medici was not destined merely to look after the family's interests in Florence on behalf of his uncle. In the preceding forty years, since the time of Sixtus IV, all of the popes' nephews (or, in the case of Alexander VI, sons) had served as commanders of the

Papal army, and there was no reason to think that it would be any different for Lorenzo, who was indeed assigned the same responsibility in 1515 (after a short tenure of the ailing Giuliano). In short, in writing to him, Machiavelli knew that he was very likely addressing a future general, even if Lorenzo was still inexperienced and patently in need of a guide.

It is in light of this project that the three decisive chapters (6, 7, and 8) of *The Prince*'s initial part must be read. In the first of them, Machiavelli praises the statesmen who were also great military commanders—such as Moses, the legendary Athenian king Theseus, the Persian emperor Cyrus, the legendary Roman king Romulus, and, at a more modest level, the third-century-BCE prince of Syracuse Hiero II—and contrasts them with a recent example: the "unarmed prophet" Savonarola, who wrongly believed that it was enough to provide for Florence's civic institutions without endowing himself with an army. Chapter 7, on the other hand, introduces the treatise's main positive model: Cesare Borgia, the son of Alexander VI, who ten years earlier had found himself in exactly the same position as Lorenzo (something the Medici knew well, as their private correspondence copiously proves). The young Borgia had never been under any illusions about his own real strengths, and so he had prepared himself well in advance for his father's death by establishing in Romagna a kind of conscription for his subjects and by having them trained in pike fighting. Although his efforts failed after a sequence of adverse circumstances that nobody could have foreseen, according to Machiavelli there was no better recent example for Lorenzo to follow.

Even if the analogy was evident to everybody (one might say that Lorenzo : Leo X :: Cesare Borgia : Alexander VI), in 1513 there was nonetheless something provocative in such a suggestion. Like his father before him, Cesare had asserted himself by the most unscrupulous means, not respecting any agreement and resorting to poison to eliminate his adversaries when other methods were ineffective; the storytellers and the poetic improvisers sung of imaginary pacts with the devil, murders, and incestuous affairs that had marked his family's rise and fall. For Machiavelli, however, the stubborn attachment of the cities of the Romagna to Cesare at his father's death was proof that the young Borgia had earned his subjects' loyalty, despite his unconventional tools for bringing order to a province traditionally riven into warring factions. This was exactly what Lorenzo needed to do in Florence.

Machiavelli was undoubtedly aware of the astonishment that his praise of the son of Alexander VI would provoke, and this is probably why the next chapter seems designed to make clear that his appreciation for Borgia's deeds did not bear an indiscriminate apologia for violence and treachery. In the analysis of the different origins of the "new principalities," chapter 8 is the only one that implies a moral judgment by dwelling on those who came to power through criminal actions (chapter 6 deals with princes who came to power through virtue, chapter 7 through fortune, chapters 9–10 through "fortunate cunning," and chapter 11 through either virtue or fortune). Accordingly, Machiavelli chooses two negative examples who share some distinct elements with the heroes of chapters 6 and 7. The villains of chapter 8, Agathocles and Oliverotto (one of Borgia's lieutenants, who had taken possession of the town of Fermo by deceitfully murdering the entire oligarchy of the city, including his own relatives), are two military commanders of undisputed valor whose political parables unfolded in the same places as Hiero and Cesare Borgia, namely, in Syracuse and in the eastern provinces of the Papal States. The similarities, however, end there. With their wicked endeavors, Agathocles and Oliverotto succeeded in exerting their "empire" over others, at least for some time. Yet, since they were completely uninterested in the common good and merely pursued their private advantage, they did not deserve "glory," that is, the following generations' praise, which for Machiavelli (in this case not unlike the humanists) is the ultimate goal of public life and should be Lorenzo's chief ambition as well—as *The Prince* continually reiterates.

The example of Cesare Borgia is intended by Machiavelli to convince Lorenzo that the difficult moment of seizing power requires special means and therefore that those who establish new political orders cannot avoid harsh measures; as one of his beloved Roman playwrights, Plautus, had taught him, "He who wants the kernel, must first break the shell" (*Curculio*, v. 55). Machiavelli goes so far as to suggest rather explicitly in chapters 9 and (less openly) 24 that Lorenzo should strike at the Florentine aristocrats, including those who had favored the Medici's return only because they hoped to gain further power for themselves and who are thus (likely) ready to betray them at the first opportunity, as they had already done in 1494 with his father, Piero, and in 1512 with Soderini. In order to avoid ending up like them, Lorenzo should therefore act immediately.

Such preemptive attacks against potential adversaries were commonly considered by Renaissance jurisprudence (in the wake of the enormously influential Bartolus of Saxoferrato's fourteenth-century *De tyranno*) one of the clearest indications of tyrannical government. It was no light matter, and Machiavelli knew it. When Bartolus had composed his treatise (inspired by Aristotle's description of the tyrant in *Politics* 5.11), he had planned to give the citizens a powerful instrument to bring to justice their legitimate lords, who were behaving unjustly, that is, who were promoting their own private interests instead of the common good. For a prince it was enough to commit just one of the ten typical tyrannical actions listed by Bartolus to become immediately accountable before his superior powers (the pope or the emperor), and during the fifteenth century some communities that were subjected to the pontiff in central Italy had indeed resorted to the *De tyranno* in order to persuade him to remove their wicked rulers. Quite the contrary, in departing from this authoritative juridical tradition, Machiavelli tries to prove via the example of Cesare Borgia that in particular situations a good prince can make use of a characteristically despotic tool without becoming a tyrant.

Moreover, Machiavelli knew that any Christian prince, as Lorenzo probably was, would hesitate to take some of the bloody actions suggested in *The Prince* for fear of divine punishment. It is for this reason that Machiavelli reminds Lorenzo that those who resort to violence "all at once to protect themselves from danger" and then convert it "into something as useful as possible for their subjects . . . can remedy their condition (*stato*) with God and with men" (chapter 8). The reasoning is dense but clear. First, the new prince has to lay his regime's foundations (whatever it costs); then, once a stable order is imposed, he will have time to amend the "state" (of mortal sin) in which his actions have placed him, trying to recover the lost "state" (of grace) before it is too late. Of course, there may be danger of eternal damnation, but for Machiavelli such danger is unavoidable for those who have chosen to perform in the public arena. As the Italians of the time used to say, anyone who takes on the responsibilities of government must "love his country more than his soul": that is, he must be willing to run the risk of going to hell for the good of his community (Machiavelli repeats the maxim in his *Florentine Histories* 3.7 and again in a late letter to Vettori written on April 17, 1527). In similar situations one should then stick to the lesson taught by Machiavelli to Vettori in another epistle, on February 25, 1514, shortly after composing *The Prince*: "it is better to do and repent, than not to do and repent" (taken verbatim from an erotic novella by Giovanni Boccaccio, *Decameron* 3.5.30).

We have already witnessed the importance of time in Machiavelli's thought. Alongside the *time of occasion*, when an unpredictable combination of events offers an opportunity that must be immediately seized, by adapting to the fickle needs of the moment, for him there is also the *time of necessity*, when a politician cannot choose and, in the interests of all, is called by the situation to execute morally questionable acts. This idea was only partially new. Already Roman law had long recognized the principle that, in the face of force majeure, it is permissible to deviate even from the most basic commandments of natural law; as the enormously influential Cicero had written, "let the salvation of the Roman people be the supreme law" (*De legibus* 3.8). But something similar had often been reiterated by medieval jurists, who asserted that "necessity has no law" (Gratian, *Decretum*, part 1, dist. 48), and by the humanists, who admitted that in exceptional circumstances the exercise of power requires behaviors that should normally be avoided with care—for example, Pope Pius II and Giovanni Pontano, the Neapolitan secretary and "prime minister" under the Aragonese dynasty and its leading writer (*De obedientia*, 1470, first printed in 1490; *De prudentia*, posthumously published in 1508). Moreover, analogous statements are frequent also in the Florentine *pratiche* after 1494, proving that the notion was universally accepted: "Necessity knows no law"; "We should ally with anybody who could help us in the reconquest of Pisa, the Turks included"; "In order to defend our liberty, we should not omit any mean; even if it is deceitful, let us take it, whenever we cannot find one that is less wicked"; "When necessity forces you, every discussion is useless"; etc. After all, even Bartolus had weighed the possibility of legitimate derogations to his strict probative system, albeit only in truly extraordinary situations (like Romulus's legendary killing of his brother Remus at the very moment of the foundation of Rome).

Machiavelli clearly works within this legal framework, yet compared to the writings of his predecessors, *The Prince* is much more extreme for at least three reasons. (1) In the "mirror" for Lorenzo the exception seems so widespread as to risk calling into question the rule, whereas the humanists who resorted to emergency measures were always very cautious in reiterating that in other situations princes and republics must adhere to the strictest ethical principles. (2) Machiavelli seems to play very deliberately on the lexical uncertainty of the term "state" (*stato*), which in his treatise indicates both the condition/status of predominance of the prince and of the State properly meant; as a result of this ambiguity, he finishes by granting indifferently to both the same freedom of action that was traditionally allowed only when the entire community was in serious danger. (3) Finally, whereas "necessity" was previously invoked only in defense, as a shield from a lethal threat, Machiavelli also refers to it in the case of a prince striking his *potential* enemies in order to strengthen his position, that is, moving to attack first.

Given Machiavelli's readiness to stretch the freedom of maneuver admitted by Roman law to its farthest limits, it is easy to understand the bewilderment of *The Prince*'s first readers. Taken together, these three innovations were sufficient to plant the suspicion that he was only looking for excuses to justify Lorenzo's actions. Even more important, consenting to his controversial view could potentially have broader outcomes of a ruinous kind: by conceding to the dedicatee the right to derogate so easily from moral imperatives, *The Prince* risked destroying an effective juridical instrument by which subjects could check their rulers. Simply put, if Machiavelli's ideas were accepted, condemning wicked princes would be much more difficult in the future because they could invoke "necessity" with greater ease. And this is, most probably, how Machiavelli's reputation as a friend to tyrants rapidly arose first in Italy and then all over Europe (following this line of thought, in 1667 John Milton labeled "necessity" as "the tyrant's plea" in his *Paradise Lost* 4, v. 394).

Yet things are clearly not so simple. *The Prince* is a book about the seizure of power, and it focuses on a particularly delicate moment in the life of all political formations: that is, when the old order is dead but the new one is struggling to be born—exactly the situation in which Florence found itself in 1513. It is here, and only here, on the uncertain threshold between night and day, that Machiavelli fixes his gaze, trying to establish rules of conduct for a transitional phase that in his view cannot be judged by the same criteria employed to evaluate steady governments, because the difficulties of the foundation process call for a greater tolerance for unorthodox means (few words are repeated as often in *The Prince* as *nuovo*, "new"). One should not be surprised, then, to discover that for the last two centuries *The Prince* has been so often the handbook of revolutionaries who fight for a radical discontinuity with the past—on the left as well as on the right.

Instrumental Virtues

Obviously, *The Prince* does not owe its place of honor in the history of political thought to Machiavelli's short-term suggestion that Lorenzo should overturn his partnership with the Florentine oligarchy and with Spain. Beyond the pragmatic objectives the author may have had (for himself and for Florence), *The Prince* distills a slowly acquired knowledge of the world, and it is this seemingly timeless wisdom that established its global success and continues to make it so relevant half a millennium later.

Readers less interested in Renaissance history almost always focus on the central chapters of the treatise, where Machiavelli reviews the qualities of the good ruler (chapter 15) and discusses the value of "liberality," that is, munificence (chapter 16); "piety," that is, clemency (chapter 17); and the right to resort to deception in war, to lie and not keep your word to other princes (chapter 18)—all conventional topics on which Machiavelli, nonetheless, reaches conclusions diametrically opposed to those of his predecessors. In particular, chapters 16 and 17 proceed to a joint demolition of the first two virtues. Following the ancients, the humanists defined munificence as a reward given over and above someone's merit and clemency as a punishment that falls short of someone's guilt, and they placed both among the essential attributes of a good prince; Cicero, for example, had warned his readers against employing fear as an instrument of government, claiming that its inevitable outcome is the irreconcilable hatred of the people (*De officiis* 2.7.23). In his analysis, Machiavelli draws attention instead to the perversity of munificence and clemency, that is, their tendency to produce effects contrary to those desired. In the abstract, a generous and forgiving prince is what everyone hopes for. In the long run, however, both "liberality" and "piety" are harmful because, by emptying the coffers of the state and inducing citizens not to fear the laws, they cannot be practiced for long. Indeed, they ultimately require harsh corrective changes like increasing taxes and intensifying exemplary sentences—even though such measures will inevitably fuel the people's hatred. Therefore, Machiavelli concludes, it is better to avoid resentment by not setting expectations that cannot be met, because (contra Cicero), if subjects are not disappointed by false hopes and surprising turnabouts, nothing dictates that a feared ruler will also be a loathed one. (Regarding "cruelty" versus "piety," in a different, that is, republican, context, *Discourses* 3.19–22 would eventually take a more nuanced position.)

As usual, Machiavelli teaches his readers to ponder not just immediate but also enduring consequences. His disapproval of "liberality" and "piety," however, also has clear antiaristocratic implications that are consistent with the overall project of *The Prince* (implications that, three centuries later, French revolutionaries would grasp very well in their attacks on royal largesse). Wherever there is a court, only those who have access to the prince and can take their grievances to him benefit from his generosity and indulgence—that is, in essence, the happy few admitted to his circle of trust and their protégés. In his history of Rome Livy had already denounced the corrupting nature of "liberality" and "piety" by analyzing the conspiracy against the newborn Roman republic organized by some young comrades of the exiled King Tarquin the Proud in 509 BCE, and Machiavelli is probably elaborating on his lesson too: "They complained among themselves that the freedom of others had been changed into slavery for them: the king, they said, is a man, from whom one can, if needed, obtain the satisfaction of a right or a wrong; there is a way to have from him a favor, a benefit . . . he can distinguish between a friend and an enemy; the laws, on the other hand, are a deaf and inexorable thing, more advantageous and more useful to the weak than to the powerful" (*Ab Urbe condita* 2.3).

For Machiavelli this story bears a valuable warning for a prince like Lorenzo, who needs to arm his subjects. Given their selective nature, "liberality" and "piety" would inevitably profit just a few already privileged individuals, in the first case by redistributing upward the wealth collected from the people through taxes and in the second by fostering a sense of impunity in the "mighty." Some would be inevitably pleased by this preferential treatment, but their support would not be enough, for Lorenzo needs to win the affection of the entire citizenry—a goal that he will be able to achieve only through a new pact between rulers and ruled, one based not on special favors but on a promise of justice and security for all. No more exceptions, for anyone: just the uniform rule of law.

(It is also noteworthy that "liberality" is just one of the many economic topics discussed in *The Prince*. To mention only a few examples: in chapter 3 Machiavelli praises the advantage of sending self-maintaining colonies to newly acquired territories instead of costly garrisons, following in the Romans' footsteps; in chapter 10 he explains how to make provisions in view of potential sieges and how to avoid straining the state's finances with outright subsidies to the less well-off when the city is surrounded by the enemy; in chapter 21 he describes Ferdinand of Aragon's cunning in exploiting for his other military enterprises the subsidy that he had received from the church for a crusade against the Muslims; again, in the same chapter, he reviews the many ways to increase a province's wealth by stimulating trade and by encouraging the influx of artisans who specialize in profitable activities; etc. Unlike previous "mirrors for princes," where the economic dimension is given very little room, in his tract for Lorenzo Machiavelli shows a remarkable curiosity for questions and problems that are typically overlooked in ancient and humanist political theory—and, as we will see, this uncommon awareness will resurface in his subsequent works.)

The passages in chapter 18 on the legitimacy of fraud, betrayal, and simulation undoubtedly constitute the most famous—and scandalous—section of the whole *Prince.* Those who condemn (or celebrate) Machiavelli as the theorist of the irrelevance of ethics in politics condense these pages into a few axioms: it is not always possible to impose oneself by fighting as a "man," that is, by respecting the rules; for this reason, it is necessary to be ready to fight like a "beast" (now like a lion overcoming other animals with violence, now like a fox, which resorts to deception); once success is achieved, the winner will have to simulate and dissimulate as well as he can in order to cover his past infractions; in politics all means are allowed because, in the end, only the result counts.

Nevertheless, nothing (or almost nothing) in this summary corresponds to the truth. First of all, Machiavelli is not formulating rules for any kind of political struggle, since the discourse has shifted here from the prince's attitude toward his subjects (in chapters 16–17) to his relations with other princes and states. Observed through these lenses, the framework of chapter 18 turns out even to be very traditional. Following Cicero's *De officiis* (1.11.34), probably the ancient treatise most read and quoted by the humanists, Machiavelli starts by explaining that the law of nations recognizes the right of sovereign states to resort to arms to settle their disputes and that when there is no judge before whom the contenders can plead their suit, only war can establish right and wrong, as in an ordeal, that is, a judgment by God. In such cases, victory itself founds the new order, regardless of the quality of the proofs and the arguments put forward by either side. As Machiavelli writes (unoriginally): "in all men's actions and especially those of princes, where there is no court to address one looks to the final outcome."

Where, then, is the scandal? Of course, Renaissance readers had no difficulty grasping the reference to Cicero, but for this very reason they could not fail to be struck by the unexpected turn that Machiavelli's reasoning takes. While in *De officiis* the two types of fight (juridical and extrajuridical) are evoked only to warn that even in the case of an armed conflict one must remember that the final objective is peaceful coexistence, *The Prince* mentions them to affirm the necessity of being ever ready for a war that is now seen as the norm rather than as a painful (but sometimes inevitable) exception. Such a serene acceptance of perpetual belligerence between states is probably one of the lessons that the Italian wars taught Machiavelli, persuading him that the ruthlessness of the conflict legitimizes even those actions that were harshly condemned by previous political theory: for, if this is how republics and principalities normally behave in the international sphere, judicious politicians can only accommodate the situation, without complaining in vain that the predictable result of such a constant struggle will necessarily be a mutual lack of trust and hardening of interstate relationships (that is, exactly the opposite of the humanitarian approach advocated by Cicero). From this point of view, it is not completely unfair to reproach Machiavelli for making what in social sciences today is called a self-fulfilling prophecy, given that his conclusion that princes and republics should not have confidence in one another inevitably reinforces (if not produces) the lack of loyalty that he himself detects.

As Machiavelli writes in chapter 18, praising duplicity in dealing with foreign political powers, "if all men were good, this precept would not be good: but because they are bad and they would not keep their word with you, you too do not have to observe it with them." To be a centaur, as chapter 18 suggests, therefore means nothing other than to learn how to use these beastly devices too and to take advantage of them in the fight *with other princes and states.* This last specification is crucial: for (contrary to a cruder interpretation of this chapter), by commending Chiron and his disciples, Machiavelli does not intend to teach a universal lesson of expediency always valid for everybody in order to win clout over others more easily (that is, also in normal daily life and civic competitions for offices). Through such an allegory he simply reminds Lorenzo that there is a place and a season—what we would call today international relations—where the rules of politics are different and where you can no longer count on jurisprudence and diplomacy alone. In this regard it is worth noting the enormous difference with Erasmus, who, more or less in the same years, in his *Institutio principis christiani* (1516), tried instead to persuade his dedicatee, the future emperor Charles V, that in the future quarrels between sovereigns should be settled through the arbitration of "bishops, abbots, wise men, and authoritative magistrates, whose opinion would be much more suitable for resolving disputes than so many massacres, spoliations, and general misfortunes" (II.8). Only in this case would the animal side of the centaur become definitively useless. But it is evident that Machiavelli never took into serious consideration such an eventuality.

Reading Machiavelli through the lens of his time does not imply minimizing his novelty, but it allows us to grasp those aspects of *The Prince* that most impressed his contemporaries and that today risk passing unnoticed. More than anything else, in chapter 18 readers must have been shocked by Machiavelli's defense of simulation and deception (a position that would later be reiterated in *Discourses* 3.40–42 in the name of the safety of the republic from foreign menaces). All previous political thinkers had unanimously asserted that lies are not only ethically unacceptable but unprofitable, because sooner or later they are always discovered, with greater damage for the perjurer; as Cicero wrote, "nothing simulated can be lasting" (*De officiis* 2.12.43, echoed by Seneca, *De clementia* I.I.I). Moreover, according to the humanists (and especially Patrizi and Pontano), this was even truer for princes, as they are constantly watched and inspected by everybody, and, living their whole existence in public, they cannot hide their actual character for long. Machiavelli, by contrast, affirms exactly the opposite, stating that the fraud denounced by the ancients as both immoral and scarcely useful is no less important than strength ("those who simply act as the lion do not understand this"), because, in the end, the great majority of people is ready, and even willing, to be deluded. As a matter of fact, people "judge more with their eyes than with their hands, because everyone is allowed to see but few are permitted to touch: everyone sees what you appear to be, few feel what you are" (chapter 18). Deceit and betrayal can be questionable but work very well in our sublunary world.

In no other passage is *The Prince*'s scandalous code of pragmatism as clear as in the opening of chapter 15, where Machiavelli claims the opportunity to break with the moralizing tradition of the *specula*:

> But my intention being to write things that are useful to those who understand them, it seemed to me more appropriate to get directly to the actual truth of the thing rather than to the way it is imagined. And many have imagined republics and principalities that have never been seen or known to exist in reality. Because the distance between how one lives and how one ought to live is so great, he who leaves what is done for what ought to be done will more quickly learn how to ruin than how to be preserved.

While in the humanists' Latin writings *virtus* indicated both a set of Christian qualities and, in accordance with the usage of the ancients, the energy and vigor that politicians need in order to resist the assaults of fortune and to impose themselves, chapter 15 shows that in *The Prince* the Italian word *virtù* has lost any religious meaning. Hence, even the traditional qualities of the good ruler are put at the service of a new, entirely utilitarian, conception of princely excellence. This change is well illustrated in the development of chapter 15. Here—before contesting "liberality" and "piety" toward subjects and loyalty in international relations—Machiavelli reviews all the assets traditionally attributed to the good prince. At first, he seems to confirm the traditional picture: a readiness to give, courage, empathy, seriousness, solicitude, and religiosity remain for him desirable in any ruler. But at the very moment when *The Prince* seems to align itself with the humanists, the chain of reasoning takes an entirely new turn. In the wake of Aristotle, fifteenth-century authors had taught that the virtues support one another and that possessing some helps in achieving the others (he who dominates lust is also better equipped against gluttony, he who nourishes great ambitions hardly yields to small vices, and so on); in Machiavelli, on the contrary, each of them is perfectly independent and proceeds on its own. Somehow, his virtues à la carte have ceased to function as a system.

This "atomization" of virtues is, however, only a preamble to a more global rethinking. While in the Greek and Roman authors and in their successors possessing a virtue means assuming a permanent disposition of the soul (a stable "habitus," as Renaissance philosophers used to say), virtues in *The Prince* are instruments to be exercised according to the needs of the moment. To quote Machiavelli (concerned as he always was about being left unprepared by the unpredictable flow of events), those who govern must "learn to be not good, and to use or not use this ability as necessary" (chapter 15). But this means that there is only one valuable criterion of judgment: effectiveness. The virtues that damage the prince's ability to engage in combat are thus to be spurned whenever the situation demands it and, if anything, simulated; those that are helpful in the fight against his enemies require cultivation with the utmost diligence; and vices that are irrelevant from a political point of view must be avoided as much as possible, but without giving them excessive importance if it is too difficult to eradicate them. Nothing else. It is not surprising, therefore, that some readers have wondered whether, reworked in view of solely pragmatic goals, Machiavelli's virtues are still virtues or instead warrant some other, less honorable name.

The Art of Bonds

The Prince insists a great deal on the importance of virtue, understood above all as military bravery, force of will, and determination in the perennial struggle against the whims of the goddess Fortune. As Machiavelli writes, with an image of extraordinary violence: "I judge it to be better to be impetuous than cautious: because Fortune is a woman, and it is necessary, to keep her down, to beat her and assault her; and one sees that she lets herself be won over by the impetuous more than by those who proceed coolly. For this reason, she is always, as a woman, a friend of the young, because they are less cautious, more ferocious, and they command her more audaciously" (chapter 25, and Machiavelli would later discuss the same topic again in *Discourses* 3.44).

Politics requires a special strength of character that few leaders really possess. However, of all the lessons that *The Prince* teaches politicians of yesterday and today, none is more important than the value of autonomy (in this regard, it is necessary to clarify that even the suggestion that the ruler should found himself on the people does not mean that he should make decisions along with his subjects but that he should build a stable alliance with them based on mutual trust and profit). For Machiavelli, the initial phase of every regime requires full freedom of action, just like moments of crisis do, when a ruler is under attack and cannot leave to others the command on which his survival depends. In fact, the collapse of the "civil principality" of the Medici, who in 1494 had been abandoned by their own supporters, represents a clear warning for Machiavelli: whoever fails to take full, preemptive control will pay the price for his error when his leadership is contested (a topic discussed especially in chapter 9).

In *The Prince*, the autonomous ruler is he who has built a good "foundation," that is, above all, he who has "his own troops." The treatise always returns to this same point. Machiavelli is not content, however, with teaching Lorenzo to distinguish the forces he truly possesses from those that depend on someone else (and which are therefore not truly his); he also shows his dedicatee the road that he should take to free himself from his benefactors' tutelage (not just the Florentine aristocrats and the Spanish but also Leo X, in anticipation of the day when his uncle the pontiff will no longer be there). Cesare Borgia provides a model for Lorenzo because he immediately understood that self-reliance was his first need and was able to quickly overturn his power relations with France, which had supported his first steps, becoming more indispensable to Louis XII than the sovereign was to him. Somehow, even if in the end it was not enough, Cesare had managed to reverse (so to speak) the magnetic poles of the ties that bound him to his initial protectors—and Lorenzo should do the same to avoid remaining a puppet in the hands of the Spaniards and the Florentine oligarchy (figure 2.1).

It is not unlikely that Machiavelli developed this original perspective by reflecting on Xenophon's *Cyropaedia*, which in the Renaissance was read as the greatest ancient "mirror for princes." In his treatise Xenophon repeatedly insists on Cyrus's ability to

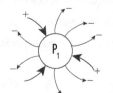

Figure 2.1. The autonomy process in *The Prince*.

draw men into his own orbit, gradually detaching them from those to whom they were previously linked (*Cyropaedia* 7.5.60; 8.1.47–48; 8.2.26–28). In particular, in light of Cesare Borgia's recent accomplishments, Machiavelli could not but be struck by a long and memorable speech in which the king of the Medes, Cyaxares, reproaches his grandson Cyrus, who was returning from a victorious campaign against the Assyrians.

Would you be happy if someone with his attentions made the dogs that you raise for the defense of yourself and your family more faithful to himself than to you? If the comparison seems weak to you, let us take another. Let's imagine that the men you have in your service to be your bodyguards and to serve in your army were placed by someone in the condition of wanting to depend on him rather than on you: would you be grateful for such a favor? ... If someone courted your wife and induced her to love him more than she loves you, would you jump for joy at his attentions? On the contrary, I don't think you could feel more bitterly offended. And if we take the example that is most pertinent to my case: if someone were to devote his care so zealously to the Persians whose leader you were, that they would follow him more willingly than you, would you treat this man as a friend? I suppose not, rather as a more execrable enemy than if he had slaughtered a good number of them! ... Now you bring me the booty you have won with my men, and you enlarge my territory with the backbone of my forces, while I, who have not contributed at all to these successes, look like a woman ready to receive gifts. All, and first of all my subordinates, look upon you as a hero,

and upon me as a ruler unworthy to command. Do you find
these to be benefits, O Cyrus?

(5.5.28–33)

In all likelihood, many of Machiavelli's reflections about the way
political ties work are indebted to Cyaxares's complaint and the
other relevant passages in the *Cyropaedia*.

Once he creates these new links (whereby he is in a position
of strength), the prince will have to learn to assess the fiber of
each and act accordingly. In fact, not all ties prove equally strong.
In particular, for Machiavelli (who on this point distances
himself from all his predecessors, including Xenophon and
Cicero), love is made of a substance much less resistant than fear,
because, while a ruler can deliberately instill fear, gratitude (a
spontaneous feeling, which for Machiavelli is synonymous with
love) cannot be imposed on others. As a result of this asymme-
try, in the case of an emergency, those who have relied too much
on thankfulness risk being disappointed, which is not the case
for those who handle the levers of power and are therefore able
to force others to remain loyal—by threats if necessary. But this
is precisely what the Medici could not do in 1494 because of
their decision to exercise only informal control over Florentine institutions.

However, even for Machiavelli fear alone cannot cement relationships between men. His point is different. As long as love
coincides with gratitude pure and simple (and the one who loves
can withdraw his gratitude at will without danger), the prince
remains at the mercy of others as soon as the fear of punishment
disappears: he must therefore make his subjects desire his success

with all their souls by making their interests converge with his own. Yet that implies a strong break with tradition. The humanists (and, again, especially Patrizi and Pontano) constantly exalted *mutual charity*—that is, the reciprocal affection between rulers and ruled when the former carry out their task well—as a basic ingredient of political obligations, but Machiavelli is not describing the same kind of bond. In fact, by transforming love into a condition of need that must be artificially inculcated in one's subjects, *The Prince* renders it an entirely different sentiment, one that has little in common with a noble passion such as genuine affection and that instead obeys the utilitarian logic of joint profit: a less elevated purpose but, in Machiavelli's eyes, one also capable of better resisting external stresses. For the good of all.

The Prince teaches that politicians *need to be needed* by their fellow citizens above all and offers them some good advice in order to make themselves irreplaceable. This was a big shift, and Machiavelli was probably the first thinker who contrasted, even shamelessly, the rationality of interests (understood as calculable desires and necessities) with the irrationality of passions (which instead remain unpredictable) and who deliberately focused on the former to give solidity to his political project. Whereas the humanists' generic appeals to virtue had failed, a different conception of human motives, perhaps less shining but certainly more realistic and above all more effective, could make a key contribution to a mission that until then had proven almost impossible. Noble sentiments are made of a more precious alloy, but one that is scarcely suitable for establishing a sound political structure, and this is the foundational goal toward which, according to Machiavelli, the wise ruler must direct all his efforts—even at the cost of opting for cheaper material. It is precisely on the basis of this idea—that we should address man "as he is" and not as "he should be" according to the philosophers and men of the church—that, in the following centuries, modern political philosophy would gradually take shape.

3

In the Garden with the Romans

Niccolò was greatly loved by them [the attendees of the Rucellai Gardens], and also generously helped with some subsidies; they took immense pleasure from the conversations with him, valuing all his writings very highly.

—Iacopo Nardi, *Histories of the City of Florence*

What If? Learning from the Past's Futures

In the last chapter of *The Prince* Machiavelli displays all his rhetorical skills in order to persuade Lorenzo to take up his project:

One must not therefore let this occasion pass, so that Italy will see her redeemer appear after so much time. Nor can I express the love with which he would be welcomed in the provinces that have suffered from these foreign floods, with what thirst for revenge, with what obstinate loyalty, with what pity, with what tears. What gates would be closed to him? What peoples would fail to obey him? What envy would oppose him? What Italian would refuse him homage? The dominion of these barbarians stinks to all. May your illustrious House therefore take up this enterprise with the heart and the hope with which just campaigns are taken up, so that under its banners this country will be made noble and, under its auspices, that saying by Petrarch will be realized:

Virtue against fury
Will take up arms, and may the struggle be short;
since the ancient valor
in Italian hearts is not yet dead.

The heated language and messianic tone are especially appropriate for a prince who is expected to fight under the banners of the church. Yet Machiavelli is not pushing Lorenzo to undertake a visionary task, for what he sees is a concrete opportunity in the favorable political conjuncture resulting from Leo X's recent ascent to the papacy. In chapter 3 of *The Prince*, Machiavelli had diagnosed a pattern in Roman conquest of Greece during the second century BCE and in the (partial and precarious) French capture of Italy in 1499–1501: when a mighty state enters a divided province, the many local powers, instead of uniting their forces to repel it, try to gain an advantage over their old competitors, only to find themselves all enslaved—a perfect case of political shortsightedness. However, now that Cardinal Giovanni de' Medici had become Leo X, the situation in Italy had unexpectedly evolved. Of the five regional powers that had governed Italy in the fifteenth century, now at least Florence and Rome were automatically on the same side, under the Medici leadership, making it finally possible to cement a broader alliance that could effectively rid the peninsula of the invaders. Of course, as long as Lorenzo and Leo did not miss this unique chance.

Things did not go this way—maybe not too surprisingly. *The Prince* was a risky bet, as Machiavelli well knew. Even if he could convince Lorenzo, it was easy to foresee the opposition of Leo X, who guided the entire family from Rome. Very likely, however, Machiavelli never got that far. On November 22, 1513, Lorenzo decided to reinstate the Council of Seventy, the oligarchic forum where from 1480 to 1494 the most important issues had been discussed; this move showed that the Medici intended to confirm their fifteenth-century alliance with the foremost families and cement their loyalty by offering the aristocrats the constitutional reform they had been craving since 1494: a Senate-led "narrow government." That choice, however, rendered *The Prince*'s "counsel" unacceptable, and after weighing for some time the possibility of adjusting his treatise in order to offer it to Lorenzo's uncle, Giuliano (as attested by his famous letter to Francesco Vettori of December 10, 1513), Machiavelli simply gave up. (This reconstruction is preferable to another hypothesis, according to which a previous dedication to Giuliano was lost and the one we read today was written at some later date.) In all probability, therefore, *The Prince* never reached any Medici desk before Lorenzo's death in 1519 (figure 3.1).

Machiavelli's correspondence in the following two years bears witness to his difficulties and discouragements. Nevertheless, transcribed in a few copies for his friends, *The Prince* helped Machiavelli emerge from isolation. The daring theses it formulated and above all the original way in which the author conducted his political analysis by comparing modern and ancient examples captured the interest of early readers, so much so that

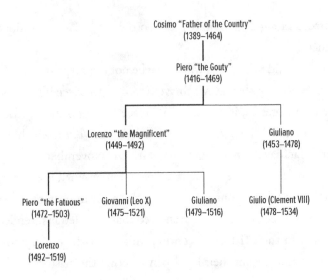

Figure 3.1. The Medici family tree.

from 1516 some of *The Prince*'s theses started appearing in the works of other Florentine authors (beginning with the young jurist and diplomat Francesco Guicciardini). A man capable of such perspicacious judgments deserved to be listened to. This is probably how it came to be that Machiavelli started attending the meetings at the Rucellai family gardens: a sort of unofficial "academy" (as some said) where, after Bernardo Rucellai's death, a new generation of aristocrats gathered to discuss literature, art, politics, history, military theory, and classicizing theater.

It is now generally agreed that the informal lectures that Machiavelli held there have some relation to the second book on which his fame rests: the *Discourses on Livy*, which was also printed only posthumously but, in the version that has come down to us, dates back to 1517–1518 and, unsurprisingly, is dedicated to two attendees of those gatherings, Cosimo Rucellai and Zanobi Buondelmonti. Whereas *The Prince* is an occasional piece of genius, the *Discourses* are undoubtedly Machiavelli's most ambitious and original work—the fruit of reflections matured over the years before being fixed in written form. For this reason, it is more difficult (and less productive) to link them to any immediate pragmatic goal, as in the case of the *speculum* for Lorenzo. Here, commenting on the first ten books of Livy's first-century-BCE history of Rome (since Petrarch's times, one of the humanists' favorite works, covering the period from Rome's legendary foundation in 753 to 290 BCE), Machiavelli discusses the most diverse issues, ranging from institutions to war techniques, from social conflicts to religion, in order to explain how the Romans built their state and nascent empire.

A grand narrative of growth, decay, and regeneration provides the general framework in which the *Discourses*' particular analyses must be located. On the one hand, following the humanists, Machiavelli divides Western history into three major phases: the classical period, a long phase of decline (the Middle Ages), and the recent revival of the arts and sciences. On the other hand, however, he notes that, while his own contemporaries attained impressive results under the guidance of the ancients in many disciplines (law, medicine, sculpture, poetry, etc.), the same was not yet true for politics and warfare. In these two areas the humanists had clearly failed, and the commentary on Livy aims precisely to instruct readers how to draw from Rome's history a series of lessons that were potentially still relevant for Machiavelli's present.

Of course, ancient history held extraordinary importance for fifteenth-century political thinkers: as Cicero taught, knowledge of the past was to be considered nothing less than "the teacher of life" (*De oratore* 2.9.36). In their treatises, though, the past was used primarily as an inexhaustible source of examples. Raised on Aristotle's writings, the humanists had no difficulty recognizing that ethics and politics had a practical, experiential dimension and that abstract principles would not suffice by themselves. In this situation, ancient (or even modern) histories provided essential aid, giving real-world scenarios to a set of rules that might otherwise turn out to be scarcely helpful, for in Greek and Roman moral and political theory virtuous conduct constantly shifts according to the given situation or the social status of the people involved (for the courage of an old man cannot be identical to that of a soldier at the height of his physical strength, and the generosity of a prince certainly differs from that of a humble peasant). With this in mind, always following Aristotle, the humanists drew not just on positive examples but also on negative ones (either by excess or by defect) in order to promote behavior that struck the coveted happy mean (e.g., teaching how to act bravely by avoiding both recklessness and cowardice or how to be liberal by being neither wasteful nor stingy). In the second case, it was a little bit like what happens in modern ballistics: where in order to hit the bull's-eye you progressively determine its exact location first with a short throw and then with a long one (in the humanists' theory: the negative examples), through a series of consecutive attempts that bring you ever closer to your target (in the humanists' theory: the positive behavior).

With Machiavelli, though, the past is no longer asked to provide anecdotes to clarify empirically the speculative doctrines of the philosophers. Instead, historians are his natural interlocutors, not for the memorable maxims or the virtuous deeds that shine in their writings but because their accounts offer readers an opportunity to practice sophisticated political role-playing—situation by situation and hypothesis after hypothesis. Why did events take a particular turn at certain moments? How could an unwanted outcome have been avoided (if it could have been avoided at all)? What can modern politicians learn from the comparative analysis of phenomena that have similar patterns although they are distant in time and space? These kinds of questions are at the core of Machiavelli's reflections both in *The Prince* and in the *Discourses*, but in the latter the procedure is made more explicit through its close analysis of Livy's narrative.

Machiavelli uses Greek and Roman historical works to explore what in today's philosophical terminology are called "counterfactual conditionals." This less observed aspect of his methodology is very important, not least because ancient political thinkers, unlike ancient historians, rarely (or never) had recourse to it. Machiavelli's treatises, on the contrary, are packed with conjectures about events that had a particular result but could have ended differently: no fewer than twenty-two passages in *The Prince* and more than one hundred in the *Discourses*, which, once put on paper, would look like today's flowcharts (although his contemporaries would have probably rather thought of some logical-rhetorical devices absorbed from the ancient philosophers and still very popular during the Renaissance, like the so-called "Porphyrian tree"). Long taught by his practical experience to weigh all the available options before opting for the "lesser evil," Machiavelli applies the same method of interrogation to the past because, in his view, bygone affairs have something to teach only if one can imagine an alternative conclusion for them—that is, exactly as the political actors of the time had perceived them when the future was still open.

In order to restore uncertainty to what is now unchangeable, Machiavelli considers it indispensable to carry out a sophisticated thought experiment, reconstructing the concrete choices that were on the table then but also exploiting the superior awareness of those who, afterward, are able retrospectively to judge and analyze the effectiveness of the decisions taken. Admiring the winners and denigrating (or pitying) the losers is useless if one does not understand why things went a certain way, nor does it enable one to identify the exact moment when the proceedings took the direction they did, as the consequence of a specific decision (right or wrong, and therefore one to be imitated or avoided). Without such a thought experiment one would risk falling back into the purely "aesthetic" and "antiquarian" attitude toward the past that Machiavelli denigrates in the proem of the *Discourses* (and later in *The Art of War*) as a sterile form of admiration for the great deeds of the ancients.

Such counterfactual inquiries into history are almost completely absent from previous political thought, whereas they are frequent in Greek and Roman historiography. Starting with Herodotus (*Histories* 7.139), to whom we owe the first counterfactual speculation ever made by a historian (regarding the Athenians' decision to face the army of the Persian emperor Xerxes rather than surrendering or emigrating westward), all the major authors from Thucydides to Tacitus had made ample use of it—including some true "bravura pieces" such as Livy's discussion of what would have happened had Alexander the Great, king of Macedonia, decided to move against Rome instead of Persia (*Ab Urbe condita* 9.17–19). Machiavelli was nevertheless the first political thinker to widely exploit these interrogations, making them one of his signature intellectual devices. And it is thanks to him alone that speculation about unrealized pasts over time became a normal tool of political analysis.

In order to understand the secret laws of history, the study of Rome offered a special vantage point: thanks to Livy, lessons could be learned from the city that had reacted best to the unexpected challenges that each community will inevitably face—both from within and from without. In other words, if scrutinizing the past is always valuable because it helps raise crucial questions in advance, Romulus and his descendants also had the significant merit of (almost always) providing the right answer. And this is why, for Machiavelli, no other city was so worthy of attention.

Machiavelli's choice of Livy proved decisive. Earlier humanist political thinkers aimed to recover the ancient philosophical tradition and to write works that could compete with those of their models both in form and content, at most either "updating" a timeless political wisdom (derived principally from Aristotle and Cicero) with some examples taken from contemporary history or further elaborating on their categories (exemplary is the example of Pontano, who in some of his treatises tried to "canonize" with Aristotelian tools social and political virtues that had not been fully investigated by the ancients, like fortitude, magnificence, or conviviality). Improvements were possible, but the key elements remained unquestioned. Machiavelli, on the contrary, disregards revered philosophical writings and turns to the practical wisdom of the Romans, that is, the principles of government that made them the rulers of the Mediterranean. Already Livy (*Ab Urbe condita* 26.22) and Cicero (*Tusculanae disputationes* 1.1.1–2) had praised Roman political expertise in contrast to abstract doctrines, and their proud statements had been occasionally repeated by humanists such as the antiquarian Flavio Biondo, Francesco Patrizi, and Bernardo Rucellai. Machiavelli nevertheless pushes this argument in favor of applied knowledge much further than anyone before him, and he uses it to promote a new kind of political theory based on the counterfactual analysis of the causes of success and failure. Therefore, by keeping foreign and domestic affairs, institutional and social dynamics, and economic and religious factors together in the same reasoning, Machiavelli came to provide a comprehensive explanation of Rome's success that was unparalleled in its complexity—a full reconstruction of what military theorists and historians now would call its "grand strategy," the highest level of statecraft, where all the aforementioned elements are taken into consideration at once in order to deploy long-term plans and preserve national security.

To apply a neologism later coined (not for Machiavelli) by the French political thinker Jean Bodin, the *Discourses* are the work of a true *philosophistoricus*, a "philosophistorian" (*Methodus ad facilem historiarum cognitionem*, 1566). It was also a pivotal shift because, by extolling the Romans' hands-on savoir faire and by rejecting the classical philosophical tradition at the same time, the commentary on Livy laid the groundwork for today's separation between political philosophers (who provide values or norms) and political scientists (who engage in value-free political discussions). But one element is especially clear: Machiavelli's famous realism has a lot do to with his seminal choice in favor of history rather than disembodied assumptions.

The *Discourses on Livy* and the "Discourse Form"

The *Discourses'* importance in the history of political thought depends no less on Machiavelli's unprecedented reading method than on their contents. Whereas *The Prince* belongs to a precise literary genre with a codified tradition, the *Discourses* are, instead, a work without any forerunner: a close reading that breaks with all the types of commentary practiced down to its own time. Machiavelli's celebration of history as the main source of political acumen required a new approach to the writings of the ancients, and this original attitude is precisely what the first readers of the *Discourses* most admired in the book. With Machiavelli's commentary on Livy, one of the true hegemonic genres of early modern political thought was born: what we may call the "discourse form." It did not take much for his friends and contemporaries to realize the significance of this breakthrough, which—though it perpetuated the cult of the ancients' deeds—proposed an innovative way of talking about politics. For instance, the Florentine historian Iacopo Nardi, a participant in the meetings held at the Rucellai Gardens, described Machiavelli's commentary on Livy as "a work certainly on a new topic and never again attempted (as far as I know) by any other author" (*Histories of the City of Florence*, posthumously published in 1582).

There is no better way to test Nardi's bold pronouncement than comparing the *Discourses* to similar works that circulated during Machiavelli's time. At the beginning of the sixteenth century the literary genre of commentary allowed for only three options—and Machiavelli's book corresponds to none of them. The first model included the scholastic expositions of the revered Greek and Islamic philosophical authorities (first and foremost Aristotle) and the glosses to writings like Dante Alighieri's *Commedia* or the sixth-century Byzantine emperor Justinian's selection of Roman jurisprudence (known as *Corpus iuris civilis*). This type of commentary was immediately recognizable for its size and format: large volumes, with the original text printed in the center of the page and methodically annotated in a smaller font in the margins. As ministers and university professors were primarily interested in the literal meaning of the hypercanonical texts they were commenting on, their first goal was to enable students and highly selected readers to understand them through a word-for-word paraphrase. Moreover, cross-references to other passages and authors that were potentially relevant for interpretation were added in the case of juridical and, sometimes, philosophical treatises, and allegorical explanations were provided wherever necessary in discussing the *Commedia* and similar compositions of great renown (figure 3.2).

More recent (but no less prestigious) was the second model: the humanistic collection of philological *castigationes*, that is, "corrections." Not only did this new kind of commentary not reproduce and rephrase the original text (which had to be found somewhere else), but it also answered different needs and had different goals. Ancient works had reached modern readers in a corrupted form, and philologists checked and amended the old

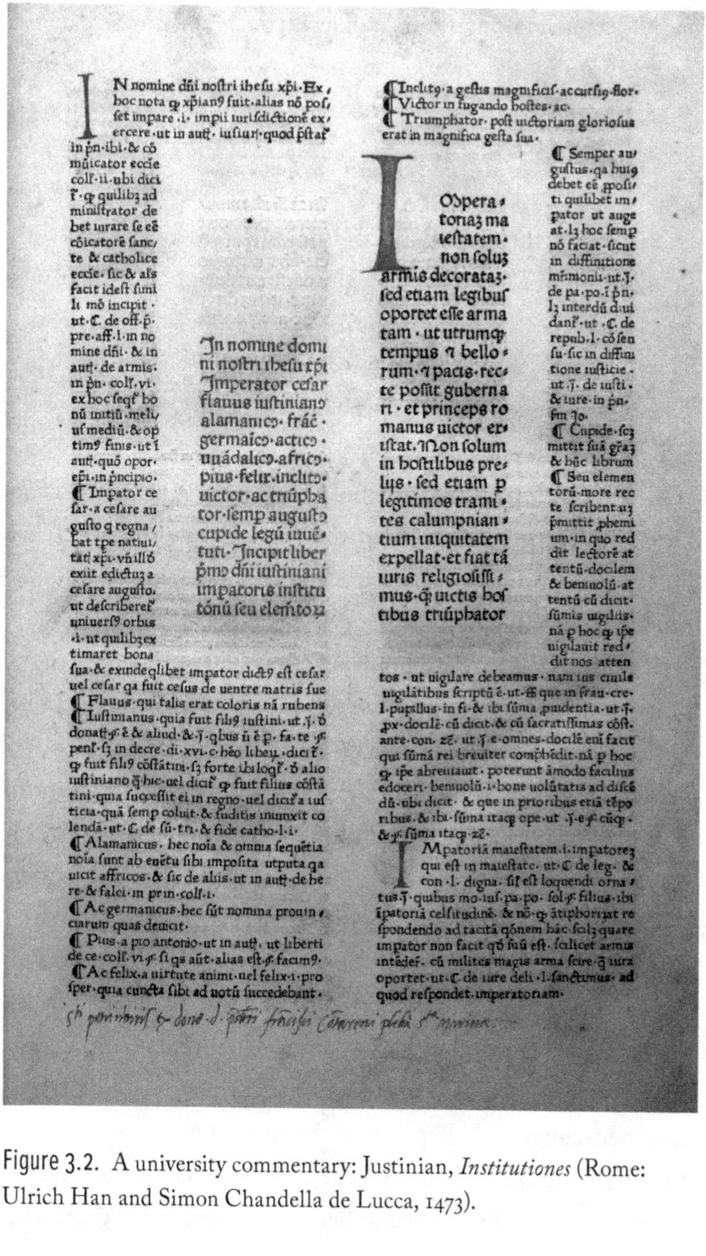

Figure 3.2. A university commentary: Justinian, *Institutiones* (Rome: Ulrich Han and Simon Chandella de Lucca, 1473).

manuscripts, making them legible again thanks to their textual conjectures; moreover, erudite elucidations were added in order to clarify ancient rituals, mythological allusions, past events and laws, the identity of a given figure, etc. Yet the emphasis on linguistic, stylistic, and historical issues was not the only difference. Unlike the university commentaries, which covered the whole work in a line-by-line fashion, their humanistic counterparts were selective and discontinuous, flexible and open-ended, as the authors of such "corrections" did not focus on every passage but discussed only the problematic points, even if remarks and corrections could be extremely numerous all the same. Such is the case of, for example, Ermolao Barbaro's *Castigationes Plinianae* (1492), with its no fewer than five thousand philological amendments to Pliny the Elder's first-century encyclopedic *Naturalis historia* (figure 3.3).

The third model is exemplified first and foremost by Angelo Poliziano's groundbreaking *Miscellaneorum centuria* (1489). Poliziano was a sophisticated philologist-poet protected by the Medici (and Adriani's mentor), and his book is in part a work of textual criticism in the tradition of the humanistic *castigationes*, although it discusses many authors at once, apparently without a recognizable order and structure, flitting erratically from flower to flower. This is not the only difference, however. Imitating the twenty-book *Noctes Atticae* by the second-century grammarian Aulus Gellius (a work widely read during the Renaissance), Poliziano organized its "corrections" in one hundred self-contained chapters on the most diverse topics, where the linguistic and textual difficulties of the manuscripts he had scrutinized in a life of study became a pretext for discussing

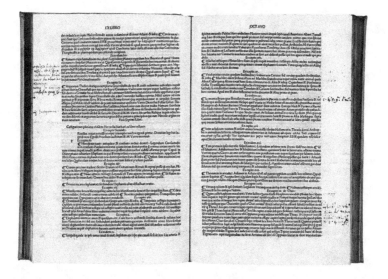

Figure 3.3. A humanist commentary: Ermolao Barbaro, *Castigationes Plinii* (Venice: Ermolao Barbaro, 1492–1493).

wide-ranging questions in the most varied fields—from theater to philosophy, astronomy to politics, numismatic to architecture, painting to religion (figure 3.4). His collection left a strong imprint on Florentine culture, and a few years later one of Poliziano's most gifted students (and early attendee of the Rucellai Gardens gatherings), Pietro Ricci, better known as Crinito, followed the *Centuria* in his *De honesta disciplina* (1504) and even radicalized Poliziano's prototype by shrinking philological analyses and by giving more room to ethical and political issues.

Where do the *Discourses* stand among these alternatives? Nowhere, for—as has been already seen—Machiavelli introduces a form of exegesis that was completely distinct from all the preexisting ones. At a structural level, contrary to the university

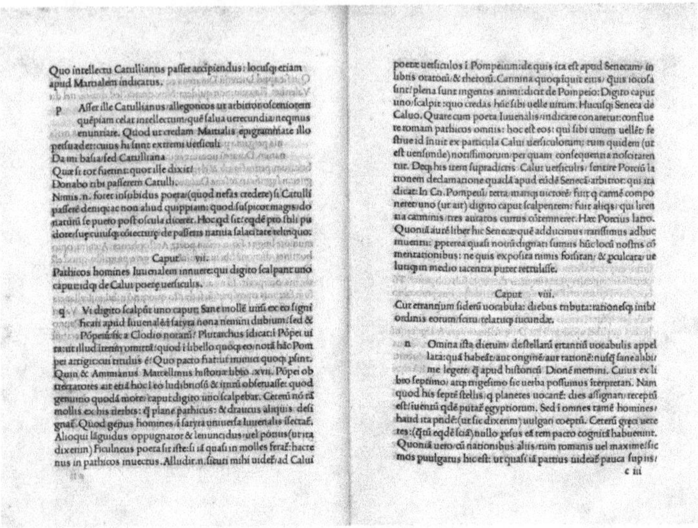

Quo intellectu Catullianus passer accipiendus: locusq; etiam
apud Martialem indicatus.

p Asser ille Catullianus/allegoricos ut arbitror/obsceniorem
quẽpiam celat intellectum/quẽ salua uerecundia/neqmus
enunriare. Quod ut credam Martialis epigrammate illo
persuadet: cuius hi sunt extremi uersiculi.
Da mi basia/sed Catulliana
Quæ si tot fuerint: quot ille dixit/
Donabo tibi passerem Catulli.
Nimis .n. foret insubidus poeta/(quod nefas credere) si Catulli
passerẽ deniq; ac non aliud quippiam: quod suspicor magis/do
naturũ se puero post oscula diceret. Hoc qd sit/eqdẽ pro sibi pu
dore/suę cuiusq; cõiecturę de passeris natiua salacitate relinquo.

Caput vii.
Pathicos homines Iuuenalem innuere: qui digito scalpant uno
caput: idq; de Calui poetę uersiculis.

q Vi digito scalpũt uno caput: Sane mollẽ uirũ ex eo signi
ficari apud Iuuenalẽ i satyra nona nemini dubium: sed &
Põpeiũ sic a Clodio notatũ/ Plutarchus idicat: i Põpei ui
ta: ut illud itidẽq; omittã/ quod i libello quoq; eo/notã hãc Pom
pei attigit: cui titulus ẽ/ Quo pacto fiat: ut inimici quoq; psint.
Quin & Ammianus Marcellinus historiæ libro .xvii. Põpei ob
trectatores ait etiã hoc i eo ludibriosũ & irrisũ obseruasse: quod
genuino quodã more: caput digito uno scalpebat. Ceterũ nõ tã
mollis ex his uerbis: q̃ plane pathicus: & draucus aliquis desi
gnat. Quod genus homines/i satyra uniuersa Iuuenalis isectat.
Alioqui lãguidus oppugnator & ieiunus idus/uel potius (ut ita
dixerim) Ficulneus poeta sit iste: si iã quasi in molles ferat: hactẽ
nus in pathicos inuectus. Alludit.n. sicuti mihi uidet/ad Calui
poetæ uersiculos i Pompeium: de quis ita est apud Senecam/ in
libris oratorũ/& rhetorũ. Carmina quoq; inquit eius/ q̃uis iocosa
sint/ plena sunt ingentis animi: dicit de Pompeio: Digito caput
uno/scalpit: quo credas hũc sibi uelle uirum. Hucusq; Seneca de
Caluo. Quare cum poeta Iuuenalis/indicare conaretur: conflue
re romam pathicos omnis: hoc est eos: qui sibi uirum uellẽt: fe
stiue id innuit ex particula Calui uersiculorum: tum quidem (ut
est uerisimile) notissimorum/per quam consequentia noscitaren
tur. Deq; his item supradictis Calui uersiculis/ sentire Porciũ la
tronem declamatione quadã apud eũdẽ Senecã/arbitror: qui ita
dicat: In Cn. Pompeiũ/ terra mariq; uictorẽ/ fuit q carmẽ compo
neret/uno (ut ait) digito caput scalpentem: fuit aliqs/ qui licen
tia carminis/tres auratos currus cõtemneret. Hæc Porcius latro.
Quoniã autẽ liber hic Senecæ: quẽ adducimus/rarissimus adhuc
inuentu: ppterea quasi notiũ dignati sumus hũc locũ nostris cõ
mentationibus: ne quis exposita nimis forsitan/ & pculcata/ ue
luti q in medio iacentia putet retrulisse.

Caput viii.
Cur errantium siderũ uocabula: diebus tributa: rationesq; inibi
ordinis eorum/situ/relatuq; iucundæ.

n Omina ista dierum/ de stellarũ errantiũ uocabulis appel
lata: quã habeãt/aut originẽ/aut rationẽ: nusq̃ sane alibi/
me legere: q̃ apud historicũ Dionẽ memini. Cuius ex li
bro septimo/ atq; trigesimo sic uerba possumus iterpretari. Nam
quod his septẽ stellis/q planetes uocant: dies assignari/ receptũ
est/ iuentũ qdẽ putat egyptiorum. Sed i omnes tamẽ homines/
haud ita pridẽ: (ut sic dixerim) uulgari coeptũ. Ceterũ gręci uete
res: (q̃tũ eqdẽ sciã) nullo prius eã rem pacto cognitã habuerunt.
Quoniã uero/cũ nationibus aliis/tum romanis uel maxime/sic
mos puulgatus hic est: ut quasi iã patrius uideat pauca sup iis/
c iii

Figure 3.4. Another kind of humanist commentary: Angelo Poliziano, *Miscellaneorum centuria prima* (Florence: Antonio di Bartolommeo Miscomini, 1489).

commentaries, the *Discourses* do not reproduce Livy's text and are highly idiosyncratic in the choice of passages they discuss, following instead the model of the humanists' *castigationes.* On the other hand, however, and in departure from the same humanists, they show no interest in examining grammatical exceptions, reviewing mythological references, or finding the most reliable versions of a religious ceremony. Contrary to the philologists, Machiavelli focuses on the facts *beyond the text*, in order to draw from *Ab Urbe condita* what he considers the richest source of political wisdom: Rome's institutional and military knowhow. And, unlike Poliziano and Crinito, not only does

Machiavelli avoid textual criticism, but his *Discourses* also analyze only a single work of a single author, so that the 142 chapters
develop a unitary line of reasoning that is very different from the
hundred independent microessays that constitute the *Miscellanea*
and from the 339 of them in the *De honesta disciplina*.

At the same time, however, Machiavelli takes something from
all of them: from the university commentaries, the emphasis on
the teaching one can draw from the glossed works (as opposed
to their mere philological correctness); from the humanists' "corrections," the selective approach to the text; from the *Miscellanea*
and the *De honesta disciplina*, the essay structure of the chapters
(so that the *Discourses* recall them at the level of the typographi-
cal organization of the page). The result is the treatise we admire
today: a meticulous reading of Livy's narrative in chronological
order that, piece by piece, assembles an interpretation of Roman
civilization as a whole, where discussions of single episodes alter-
nate with a series of chapters devoted to broader questions and to
comparative analyses of other republics, ancient (like Sparta,
Athens, or the Etruscan cities) and modern (like Venice or the
Swiss cantons).

In Machiavelli's hands, a myriad of disparate anecdotes and
apparently negligible details coalesce into a coherent system of
government, revealing what made Rome's success possible.
Renaissance readers were rightly stupefied by the depth and
breadth of such an inquiry; on the contrary, later readers risk
missing the novelty of the *Discourses*, but this is the reason
why—in order properly to understand them—it is all the more
necessary for us to recapture at least some of the initial astonishment they provoked. To learn from Rome, Machiavelli had

to invent a fresh way of going through Latin and Greek authors—and this is exactly what his commentary on Livy does in the first place, opening a new path to historical research and political theory. The dozens, if not hundreds, of imitations of the *Discourses* that were published over the next two centuries are the best available proof of the mark that Machiavelli's new methodology was destined to leave all over Europe.

Constitutional Engineering

Despite its polycentric and even eccentric structure, Machiavelli's commentary on Livy is a coherent work organized with great care in order to produce a full interpretation of Rome's political deeds. While *The Prince* investigates just the actions that a single individual must take at a particular moment—those related to the seizure of power—more ambitiously, the *Discourses* focus first and foremost on how republics ought to be arranged and ruled in the most various situations. In doing so, they offer an unparalleled analysis that ranges from domestic politics (in book 1) to foreign policy and warfare (in book 2) and, finally, examines the many ways that Roman citizens individually contributed to the success of their country (in book 3).

Especially in the first part of book 1 Machiavelli engages in a dialogue with a long tradition of thought that starts with the ancient Greeks and identifies the different forms of government as the single element most capable of explaining the success or failure of republics and kingdoms past and present. From the thirteenth century onward, political theorists had relied primarily on the lessons of Aristotle, who during the Middle Ages and the Renaissance was considered the source of all wisdom in any discipline (to the point that Dante called him "the teacher of those who know" in *Inferno* 4, v. 131). In his much-read *Politics* Aristotle identifies six basic constitutions, distinguished by the number of rulers and their attitude—either virtuous or corrupt according to the ends they pursue (in the first case the common good, in the second their private interests). The three virtuous forms are monarchy (the government of one), aristocracy (the government of the few), and polity (the government of the many), while the three corrupt forms correspond to tyranny, oligarchy, and democracy. But this is just the basic scaffold, for, through a large number of examples, Aristotle analyzes the strengths and weaknesses of each of the constitutional forms (even tyranny), showing how they could be rendered more stable and drawing from their comparison general considerations about what works in politics and what does not.

The first teaching of Aristotle is probably that there is no absolutely preferable constitution: as the Persian Empire demonstrates, not all communities are suitable for the self-government practiced by the Greeks. However, at least in the abstract, according to his *Politics* the best form is monarchy and the worst tyranny, while the least bad is democracy (since here the interest of the many coincides with that of the majority, which is closer to the common good). When it comes to free republics, extremes must be carefully avoided; for this reason, an intermediate constitution capable of combining aristocracy and polity and of gaining broad middle-class support deserves particular praise. Moreover, involving many citizens in governance also ensures sounder judgment, because a plurality inevitably assesses a situation better than one or a few. As for tyranny, it is both the worst and most precarious political form: destined as it is to collapse, and soon, under the weight of its own defects (if it does not evolve first into a virtuous principality).

Ever since Aristotle's *Nicomachean Ethics* and *Politics* were translated into Latin (around 1250 and 1260, respectively), thinkers all over Europe had adopted his categories, sometimes enriching and correcting them, but without modifying the general framework—although this framework was occasionally supplemented by some ideas taken from Plato, for example, the possibility of assembling a sort of superconstitution by mixing monarchy, aristocracy, and popular rule. In respect to this tradition, Machiavelli fleshed out a completely different theory, originally drawing on the analyses of two Greek historians who had only recently been rediscovered in the West: the *Histories* by Polybius of Megalopolis and the *Roman Antiquities* by Dionysius of Halicarnassus. It was a major swerve in the history of European political thought and one that still today profoundly affects how we think about the functioning of our democratic institutions. For this reason, special attention has to be given to how Machiavelli creatively reworked his Greek sources in his own theory.

Polybius (c. 200–118 BCE) came to Rome as a hostage at the time of the conquest of Greece, and there he became an admirer of the institutions of a city that—after its victory over Carthage in the Second Punic War (218–202 BCE)—was well on its way to dominating the entire Mediterranean basin. For this reason, Polybius chose to analyze the causes of Roman success in a vast historiographical work of forty books (spanning 264 to 146 BCE, when Carthage was definitively annihilated), of which only the first five survive in full (reaching down to 220 BCE). The sixth

book (in Machiavelli's time available in Latin only in a manuscript version) contained a digression in which the Roman constitution was compared to those of the most famous ancient
republics (Athens, Sparta, and Carthage) and commended for
its perfection. According to Polybius, while the six basic political forms are unstable and constantly supplanted by one another
(moving from monarchy to tyranny, from tyranny to aristocracy, from aristocracy to oligarchy, from oligarchy to democracy,
and from democracy to ochlocracy, or mob rule—and from
there proceeding in a sort of "circle" back to monarchy), the
Romans adopted a steady combination of monarchy (the consuls), aristocracy (the senate), and democracy (the assembly),
that assured them victory against Carthage. Thanks to a similar
mix (resembling Plato's superconstitution), Sparta, too, had for
some time imposed itself on the other Greek cities, but it had
not achieved the same results as Rome because, in order to avoid
internal quarrels, its legendary legislator Lycurgus had banned
all precious metals. As a result, when centuries later Sparta
found itself thrust upon the international stage, its lack of gold
and silver prevented its expansion.

Dionysius of Halicarnassus (c. 60–7 BCE) came to Rome a
century later, in the age of Emperor Augustus. He too set out
to explain Rome's success to his compatriots, and, to this end,
he reclaimed Polybius's legacy by composing a twenty-book history covering the years from the city's legendary foundation in
753 BCE to 264 BCE, precisely where Polybius's narrative begins
(the first ten books, the only ones surviving in their entirety,
cover the period to 447 BCE and had been translated into Latin
between 1449 and 1469/70). Unlike his model, however, Dionysius did not condense all his considerations on Roman institutions

into a single book but scattered them throughout the whole work, often putting the acutest analyses in the mouths of major historical figures (kings and senators, tribunes of the plebs, and consuls) to give his readers an idea of what was at stake at any turning point of his narrative.

The originality of Polybius's and Dionysius's approach lies crucially in the fact that, unlike the six basic forms of government, their mixed constitution resembles the gears of a complicated mechanism whose many elements—either single magistrates or deliberative bodies—reveal their functions only when they are observed in relation to one another and to the whole. Hence, for both of them, you cannot just list the many elected officers and explain what each of them does (as Aristotle does): you have to show the readers their multiple (and often conflicting) interactions. This is the principal lesson that Machiavelli learned from the two Greek historians—a lesson that, carefully reconsidered, allowed him to inaugurate modern constitutional engineering, with its special attention to the many checks and balances necessary to produce and preserve freedom. It was a major innovation that eventually led political thinkers to develop the theory of the separation of executive, legislative, and judicial powers on which, since the eighteenth century, modern fundamental laws have been based all over the world, starting with the United States in 1787–1789. A long history began with Machiavelli's theory of "mixed government." But without Polybius and, above all, Dionysius, there would be no *Discourses*—at least as we know them.

The *Discourses'* focus on the cogs that make institutions work is anything but surprising, for throughout his life Machiavelli never ceased thinking about liberty and power in terms of connections, and his analysis of Roman magistrates and deliberative bodies has a clear precedent in *The Prince*'s insistence on political links. Nonetheless, in the commentary on Livy the prior perspective is somehow reversed. In discussing the founding of a new regime, *The Prince* advised Lorenzo that autonomy must be his first and foremost goal and that he should rebuild previous bonds in order to put himself at the center of a new network of relationships from a position of strength. Quite the opposite, the *Discourses* warns readers that freedom depends on mutual ties rooted in institutions and that only if these ties are robust enough can republics truly prosper. In one form or another, to preserve liberty, every citizen (and especially every officer) must be bound by laws and constantly checked in his dangerous antisocial appetites. It is therefore with this preoccupation in mind that Machiavelli even comes to write that lawgivers should "presume everybody guilty" when they devise the future constitution of their city (*Discourses* 1.3), provocatively reversing the basic principle of Roman jurisprudence that all shall be considered innocent until proven culpable. Licentiousness (that is, the absence of any restraint) is no less remote from freedom than servitude and therefore must be contrasted at any cost.

For Machiavelli, the control that magistrates exert over one another plays an essential role because, unlike the humanists, he does not believe that an enlightened pedagogy based on the reading of the classics will free men completely from their selfish desires—or at least he does not believe that the liberty of all can be entrusted to the education of the few when so many examples of the past have shown that the best training by the best teachers hardly guarantees a ruler's disinterested commitment to the public good. Any unregulated power risks turning into despotism, regardless of the moral and intellectual qualities of those who exercise it, and it is here that constitutional engineering comes into play as the science of the bonds that advance (or hurt) republican liberty.

In a few years, the *Discourses* profoundly reshaped how forms of government (and politics in general) were discussed. New questions arose, and ancient analyses became much subtler. Yet Machiavelli's promotion of the mixed constitution also had unforeseen consequences. During the fifteenth century, political thinkers had not distinguished much between Rome, Sparta, and Athens, which were generally appreciated or criticized en masse according to each author's preference for republican or princely rule. In the wake of Machiavelli (and also of Polybius and Dionysius), it became normal instead to sharply distinguish simple constitutions, such as Athens, from mixed constitutions, such as Sparta and Rome, by placing them on two distinct levels. Thus, while among the humanists (Leonardo Bruni, Cyriac of Ancona, Lauro Quirini, Francesco Patrizi, Filippo Beroaldo the Elder, Mario Salamonio degli Alberteschi, etc.) there was no shortage of sincere admirers of Athens's institutions (especially in its earlier, more oligarchic configuration as crafted by the lawgiver Solon in the sixth century BCE), after the *Discourses* political theorists started placing good democracy (or, according to Aristotle's terminology, polity) among the forms of government that were not to be imitated (in any version). After Machiavelli, for the great majority of republican political thinkers, only Sparta and Rome had enjoyed a blameless constitution. In this way, the *Discourses* fueled a general condemnation of Athens's political experience that would last until the eighteenth century, when, in a new cultural context, a reevaluation of its democratic history and principles would gradually take place.

In the Footsteps of Dionysius

Tracing the ways in which Machiavelli reworked the *Roman Antiquities*' lessons to build his own political theory is probably one of the best approaches to the *Discourses*. Although he never mentions either Polybius or Dionysius, Machiavelli certainly meditated on them both, even if it was the latter who exercised the greater influence on him. Not only do the *Roman Antiquities* cover exactly the same events as Livy's first books (therefore providing Machiavelli with many minor insights valuable to his own commentary), but every time the *Discourses* diverge from Polybius in their analysis of the Roman constitution, they coincide with Dionysius's. For instance, unlike Polybius, both Dionysius and Machiavelli thought the foundations for "mixed government" were laid by the legendary king Romulus, who already in 753 BCE shared his power with the Senate and with the citizens' assembly; all six simple forms (including monarchy, aristocracy, and democracy) are bad because of their scarce durability; the popular element of Rome's institutions is to be recognized not so much in the assembly (which was already present in Romulus's original constitution) but in the tribunate of the plebs, which was introduced only later, in 494 BCE (and is completely absent from Polybius); institutional stability does not stem from the mutual need for collaboration between the many officers and political bodies but from the power of vetoes (and the judicial threats) that they can exercise over others; and so on.

Under the *Roman Antiquities'* influence, the *Discourses* resemble, so to speak, a cross-eyed commentary: where Machiavelli adopts as a base text one of the most beloved (and canonical) classics—Livy's *Ab Urbe condita*—but in its inquiry constantly takes advantage of a second, alternative version of the same events and of its concurrent explanations. Tellingly, the main difference between Livy's and Dionysius's understanding of early Roman history concerns the weight of institutions. While Livy, like all Roman historians, tends to illuminate the success and failure of states in terms of moral virtue and has little to say about the complex set of rules and procedures through which Rome was governed, Dionysius insists rather on the merits and demerits of each constitution, largely tracing even citizens' qualities (or vices) back to the fundamental laws of their country—a perspective that Machiavelli deftly incorporates in his own interpretation.

Three examples will suffice to give an idea of how relevant Machiavelli's debt to the *Roman Antiquities* is and of the original ways in which he absorbed Dionysius's lesson.

I.   Following Aristotle (*Politics* 7.4), throughout the fifteenth century humanists never ceased to repeat that cities must be careful not to exceed an ideal size in order to minimize the potential for internal conflict. In the wake of Cicero (*Pro Cornelius Balbus* 13 and 22) and Tacitus (*Annales* 11.24), some antiquarians, such as Biondo in his ten-book erudite reconstruction of Roman civilization (*Roma triumphans*, 1459, first printed in 1473), had occasionally acknowledged that the Romans' generosity in welcoming newcomers and, later, assimilating peoples defeated in war was responsible for their success, but these authors had never drawn from this fact any general lesson. It was Machiavelli who turned the Roman example into a universal law of history, according to which open republics prosper while closed ones court ruin. After 1494, in light of the disasters caused by the power differential between Italy's regional states and the recently consolidated monarchies in France and Spain, it was impossible to be pleased with the evident similarities between the Italian communes and the Greek cities, as the humanists had often been in the past (to give a simple example, around the year 1500, the ratio between the population of all the Florentine dominions in Tuscany, 450,000 inhabitants, and that of the Kingdom of France, 16 million, was approximately 1 to 35: greater than the ratio that exists today between France or Italy and China). Simply put, for Machiavelli, more citizens mean more soldiers—but all the fundamental elements of his reasoning are already in the *Roman Antiquities* (1.9; 2.16–17; 3.10–11; 4.22–23; 6.19), which had given much room to the Romans' efforts to remedy their initial weakness (for example, the legendary Rape of the Sabine Women and Romulus's equally legendary opening of an asylum for newcomers) and had even drawn an elaborate comparison with the disastrous outcomes of the Greek cities' closure that Machiavelli closely takes up in *Discourses* 2.4. If, to everyone's surprise, Rome was able to recover from the defeat inflicted by the Carthaginians at Cannae (216 BCE) while neither Athens nor Sparta nor Thebes ever succeeded in establishing a lasting hegemony over Greece, it was in fact just because, unlike the

Romans, Greek citizens were too jealous of their privileges and never understood that only by integrating alien populations could their republics grow stronger. Dionysius's comparison therefore contained strong advice for the future, advice that—through the *Discourses*—would exert a persistent influence, including on the laws of the United States regarding immigrant naturalization (as proved by the Founding Father James Wilson's explicit mention of Machiavelli on this aspect in his *Lectures on Law*, posthumously published in 1804).

2. Any reader of Livy knows the importance that is attached to social conflicts and the first-order role that the tribunes of the plebs played in his history. The tribunes were the defenders of the Roman people, elected from among the nonpatricians only, and (after the plebs' secession to Mount Marius in 494 BCE) endowed with considerable power, including the right to veto any law, stop military conscription, and incriminate before the assembly any citizen suspected of harming the republic's freedom. However, being also the leaders of the popular faction, the tribunes were often blamed for the divisions of Rome in the ancient sources (e.g., Cicero, *De legibus* 3.8–10; Florus, *Epitoma* 2.1—but Livy too can be very bitter with them), and the humanists unanimously echoed this hostile attitude. A notable exception was nonetheless Dionysius (*Roman Antiquities* 4.73–74; 7.55–56; 7.65–66), whose favorable judgment is significantly endorsed in full by Machiavelli. As a matter of fact, both in the *Roman Antiquities* and in the *Discourses* the tribunes (not the assembly) constitute the democratic element of Rome, which became a stable "mixed government" only after the final ratification of their powers by the Senate in

490 BCE (*Discourses* 1.2–5). Moreover, Dionysius and Machiavelli highly praise the popular trials that ancient thinkers had always criticized (starting with Aristotle, *Politics* 6.5), because they both see the tribunes' power of indictment as an indispensable tool not just for protecting the plebeians from the patricians' abuses but also for preserving the liberty of the republic by making all citizens more virtuous through the threat of legal action before the assembly (*Discourses* 1.5 and 1.7–8). Such unusual appreciation for the tribunate is without any doubt one of the most original traits of Machiavelli's republicanism, but in this case too Dionysius's influence is clearly detectable.

3. Besides the tribunes, another magistrate is absent from Polybius's reconstruction but central to both Dionysius's and Machiavelli's: the Roman dictator. Humanists were unsure exactly how to describe this emergency magistracy, which was endowed with extraordinary powers (it was impossible to appeal against his decisions) but which was bound also to respect the republican institutions (and was appointed by the Senate for only six months, instead of twelve, like the two consuls and the majority of the Roman magistrates). Above all, dictatorship suffered from a universally bad reputation after Lucius Cornelius Sulla and Julius Caesar had exploited the title to cover up their unconstitutional authority during the civil wars of the first century BCE, and the humanists had voiced this criticism. Machiavelli, however, could read in Dionysius lengthy praise for the many advantages that briefly concentrating all the power in one man had long afforded Rome, before Sulla and Julius Caesar perverted it (*Roman Antiquities* 5.70–77). Sensitive as he was to unforeseen dangers (and to the ways

of reacting to them), Machiavelli enthusiastically approved this atypical view, with the effect that—following the *Roman Antiquities*—the *Discourses* became the first modern political work to commend the Roman dictatorship: both as an exceptional (but legal) response to especially serious threats (*Discourses* 1.34) and as a potential way out of the many stalemates that risk paralyzing a mixed constitution, such as (for example) if the two consuls are in disagreement (1.50).

Citizenship right–tribunes–dictatorship: Dionysius's analyses constantly resurface at the heart of the *Discourses* (figure 3.5). No other author was probably so important to Machiavelli (excluding Livy). The *Roman Antiquities*' influence, however, is not limited to the understanding of Roman institutions alone and involves at least another major issue—as we will now see.

Positive Conflicts (and Other Brilliant Ideas)

That unity makes strength is an intuitive concept on which the ancients and humanists never ceased to insist, condemning internal divisions in the name of civic harmony. All for one, one for all: who would disagree? Nevertheless, in the opening chapters of the *Discourses* (1.4–6), Machiavelli explicitly takes a stance against this idea in bold defense of Roman tumults (and more generally of social conflicts)—a position that would be remembered as one of his most original and controversial statements, as well as a genuine watershed in Western political theory. During the fifteenth century, Rome had often been

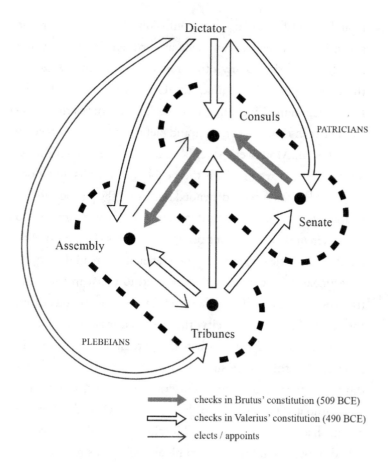

Figure 3.5. Roman constitution according to Dionysius of Halicarnassus (and Machiavelli).

criticized by humanists for the struggles between the patricians and the plebeians; hence, Machiavelli may have felt obliged to forestall at the outset any potential objections to his claim that the moderns should take inspiration from the Romans. To those who had accused Rome of "having been a tumultuous republic, and full of so much confusion, that if good fortune and military virtue had not made up for their defects, it would have been inferior to any other republic" (1.4), the *Discourses* therefore replied that, unlike the Greek cities (and later the Italian communes, including Florence), for centuries the struggles between Roman patricians and plebeians had never taken a violent turn. Moreover, Machiavelli insists, "every city must have its own ways in which the people can vent its ambition" (1.4), and Rome's success depended largely on the people's ability to force the richest and most powerful citizens to give in to their demands without ever resorting to arms. Endowed with admirable political creativity, the plebeians instead developed other means: for example, they refused to enlist in the army (the so-called *detractio militiae*) and, in the most serious cases, they even abandoned the city (the so-called *secessio*), exploiting external military threats to win the patricians' opposition (in reverse, something very similar to what Florentine aristocrats did when they refused to underwrite new loans, leaving the city without the possibility of hiring an army). Only after the Senate had had the brothers Tiberius and Gaius Gracchus killed without trial in order to block their plans to redistribute land (in 133 and 121 BCE) did blood begin to flow in Rome, too, but the civil wars that overcome the republic, being triggered by ambitious generals (like the aforementioned Sulla and Julius Caesar) and fought by their legions, had nothing in common with the protests of the first centuries. Indeed, before the Gracchi were murdered, the conflict of the Orders had generated considerable benefits, beginning with the tribunes of the plebs, which made Rome a "mixed government" for the good of the whole community.

Machiavelli's surprising and provocative apologia for Roman tumults has just a single precedent among classical authors: Dionysius, once again. In fact, the *Roman Antiquities* offered a clear distinction between the good conflicts that were part of Roman republican life in its early stages and their later degenerations (7.65–66) and also provided a lengthy comparison between Roman and Greek internecine strife, making a strong argument in defense of Rome's almost bloodless struggles (for, as Machiavelli points out, in three or four centuries only a handful of Romans were killed by riots in the streets). This is a brief passage, but one that Machiavelli exploited with great intelligence for his own purposes. In book 3 of the *Roman Antiquities*, Dionysius tells of the contrast that arose between Rome and its ancestor Alba Longa, and the decision of their sovereigns, Tullus Hostilius and Mettius Fufetius, to avoid a war between cognate peoples through a duel that would decide which of the two populations would relocate into the other city (this is the origin of the famous legend of the Horatii and Curiatii). In the speeches that precede the fight, Mettius Fufetius praises the purity of Alba Longa's lineage, which, unlike Rome, had not given shelter to newcomers and was therefore not plagued by internal conflicts. To this attack Tullus Hostilius responds with an eloquent defense of the Roman model, with its openness to foreigners, its mighty army, and even its social unrest: "The power of the cities resides in their military strength, but military strength depends on the abundance of men. . . . Your city, starting from remarkable fame and great wealth, has shrunk to a small center; we, on the contrary, from a modest origin, in a very short time have made Rome the largest center in the area, and precisely by doing what you condemn. Our internal discords, since you reproach us for them, do not lead to the overthrow and weakening of the state, but to its recovery and growth" (*Roman Antiquities* 3.11).

We have already seen that Machiavelli (following Dionysius) establishes a precise nexus between population and military force; it is therefore not surprising that he was fascinated by Tullus Hostilius's arguments to the point of making them his own (not to mention the fact that somebody like him, who had been discriminated against by Florence's laws on illegitimate procreation, also had personal reasons to disapprove of Alba Longa's foolish efforts to preserve its presumed ethnic integrity). For Machiavelli, the Roman plebs deserved recognition for its avoidance of violence, but in his view the most important thing that any republic must learn is how to manage social effervescence (and even antagonism) without eliminating it altogether. Machiavelli highlights this idea first of all by referring to the different social groups as "humors"—a technical term derived from Hippocrates, the great fifth-century-BCE Greek physician and "father" of ancient medicine. Renaissance science did not know about viruses and bacteria and stated that all diseases depended on an imbalance (*dyscrasia*) of the four basic components of the body: black bile, yellow bile, phlegm, and blood. Sixteenth-century belief held that the predominance of any of these fluids was capable of triggering a variety of sicknesses and that any such lack of equipoise therefore had to be promptly corrected, if necessary, with a special diet or with substances that would help the patient expel excessive fluids through sweat, mucus, urine, vomit, or diarrhea and so recover the right equilibrium (*eucrasia*). By turning repeatedly to this image, Machiavelli suggests that something similar applies to states—with two important consequences. First, by equating social groups with "humors," the *Discourses* recognize that it is impossible to dispense with conflicts because social classes, like body fluids, constantly seek to prevail over one another (in Machiavelli there is no such thing as the stabilizing government of the middle class that had been so popular among the fifteenth-century humanists inspired by Aristotle). Health is therefore envisioned as something quite like a moment of respite in a sequence of consecutive imbalances, with the result that perfect harmony is illusory at best, pathological at worst. The second corollary of Machiavelli's medical metaphor is that none of the "humors" of which the city is composed may be, or should be, eradicated. In this analogy with the human body, the well-being of the republic is not in fact associated with the quiet that accompanies the secure ascendency of the people or of the "mighty" (let alone the complete removal of the rich, along the lines of Marxist class struggle) but rather with their dynamic (and precarious) steadiness. And this means that, despite Machiavelli's evident pro-popular sympathies, his defense of Roman tumults implies no revolutionary project; quite the contrary, by venting social tensions in nondangerous forms, well-regulated conflict can even have the effect of strengthening the ruling regime, thereby preventing change (an idea that would be valorized by some of Machiavelli's seventeenth-century Italian followers). Wise politicians have to devise ways to make social strife innocuous, not attempt to eliminate it.

This appreciation for (relatively) bloodless Roman tumults does not, of course, exclude the possibility that, in particular situations, other remedies may be necessary—just as Renaissance medicine contemplated surgery for the most obstinate ills. Machiavelli dwells on them especially in *Discourses* 1.9–10, where he introduces the figure of Cleomenes III, the third-century-BCE Spartan king and social reformer who tried to restore the sumptuary decrees imposed by the legendary lawgiver Lycurgus. In order to solve the social crisis in which his city had long been embroiled and to bring it back to its ancient military strength, Cleomenes first cleared away the opposition by putting his aristocratic adversaries to death before they could hinder him in his designs, and only the armed intervention of Macedonia in Greece impeded his project. It was the right thing to do in that situation. According to Machiavelli, the Gracchi, on the other hand, had shown poor judgment when, in their attempt to remedy Rome's economic disparities (and in particular to counter the spread of landed estates that were destroying the citizen army's social foundations), they had deluded themselves that the usual means of pressure would be enough to have their reforms approved by the Senate. What they failed to understand was that, since this particular conflict was fundamentally economic and did not concern, as in the past, only the plebeians' legal recognition and civil rights, the patricians would have never complied with such a deep transformation in the power relations: simply put, in this case there was no possibility of agreement. For this reason, as Machiavelli writes, "one should praise the intention more than the prudence" of the two brothers (1.37), that is, their aims rather than their ability to identify the appropriate means to achieve them. The Gracchi were crushed because they had hesitated in the face of violence, while—given Roman society's advanced degree of corruption—they should have remembered the lesson of Hippocrates about severe diseases that require the surgeon's scalpel: "Desperate times call for desperate measures" (*Aphorisms* 1.6).

This idea entails a more general principle. For Machiavelli any political and social organization tends to degenerate over time, and the only way to make it last is periodically to return to its point of origin, when the citizens were more virtuous because they feared the absolute power of the lawgiver. That is what the Romans did whenever they appointed a dictator but also what the Medici did in Florence during the fifteenth century, when every five years they selected a special commission of trusted men to strengthen their grip on the city before their adversaries could start plotting against them. Elsewhere Machiavelli even states that the only reason the church has lasted for so many centuries is because Saint Dominic and Saint Francis operated in the same way, by returning to the "first principles" of Christian religion and setting in motion a process of moral regeneration of the believers (*Discourses* 3.1). Aging and corruption are an element of both natural and artificial bodies, but, while in the first case nothing can stop the ordinary process of decay, for Machiavelli political institutions can be rejuvenated at least in part to make them last longer. To this end, it may be necessary to concentrate all power in the hands of a single reformer (as Cleomenes did), although there is a considerable risk in this process, for nobody can predict whether the leader called to reshape the institutions like a new lawgiver would remain loyal to republican freedom or would abuse his temporary unchecked authority to impose a permanent tyrannical rule over the city (1.18: the entire chapter can be read as a melancholy and disillusioned self-commentary on *The Prince*'s political project after its failure). Only his subsequent actions will tell, but it is important to acknowledge the potential danger—even if sometimes running the risk may be unavoidable.

The defense of social conflict is so important to Machiavelli that it leads him to reformulate in a completely original way the theory of "mixed government" as derived from Polybius and Dionysius. In the *Discourses* mixed constitutions are divided into two large families based on their attitude toward newcomers and, consequently, on their military capabilities. On the one hand there is Rome: pro-popular, ready to grant citizenship to immigrants and subjugated populations, and, as a consequence, densely inhabited and armed—but inevitably dogged by internal conflict, because a fighting people claims the right to participate in the government of the city and the constant influx of aliens makes social harmony more difficult to maintain. On the other hand, there are Sparta and, among the modern republics, Venice: pro-aristocratic and socially peaceful because they are hermetically sealed off from the external world and reluctant to enlist their own citizens, but for these same reasons also lacking the military force necessary to protect and expand their domains. Each of these options obviously has its advantages, and one might dream of seeing them blended in a sort of mixed superconstitution, invincible on the outside and at peace on the inside. Yet this combination is a pipe dream, as the *Discourses* immediately make clear, for Rome's and Sparta/Venice's different strengths (military power and social concord, respectively) are merely the outcomes of their opposite choices regarding citizenship.

In the end, Machiavelli has no doubt: in spite of the almost unconditional admiration that Venice enjoyed among the humanists and, more generally, his own contemporaries (especially the Florentine aristocrats), the Roman constitution seems so preferable that its tumults should be considered at most "a necessary inconvenience" (*Discourses* 1.6)—which is more or less what Tullus Hostilius had replied to Mettius Fufetius in the *Roman Antiquities*. Since war is not always chosen, aristocratic mixed constitutions can be forced into a fight even if they do not want it, but also in the very unlikely event that a republic arranged like Sparta and Venice could really avoid becoming embroiled in any confrontation with its neighbors, Machiavelli notes that prolonged peace would gradually make it unable to defend itself, thereby exposing it to certain ruin in the long run. A mixed constitution such as Rome's can instead elect not to conquer (at least in theory) while still being ready for any war that others mount against it. In short, there is no real alternative: for Machiavelli the only model worthy of imitation is the Roman one (figure 3.6).

How Republics Die

No matter how valuable it is to restore a republic by returning it to its "first principles" (*Discourses* 3.1), sooner or later every artificial body is bound to perish. Machiavelli knows that, and he accepts this law of life without expressing much distress ("It is impossible to found a perpetual republic," as we read in 3.16). Had the Gracchi succeeded in their plan, civic freedom might have lasted longer, but because the two brothers chose the wrong tools and were defeated, Rome set off down the road toward imperial rule. But it was just a matter of time, because—in one way or another and for every state—the future is doomed (Machiavelli must have also remembered Lucretius's lesson: "All things gradually decay and go to the

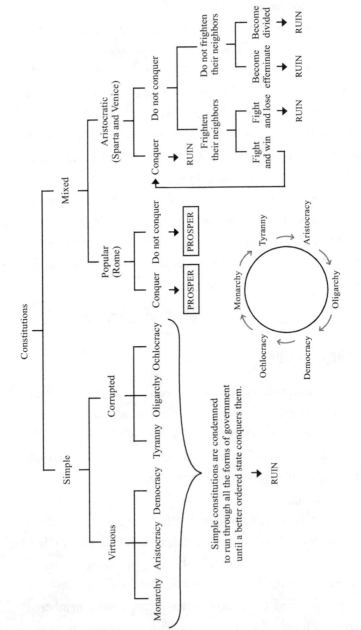

Figure 3.6. Constitutional forms according to Machiavelli (*Discourses* I.2–6). The ring illustrates Polybius's and Machiavelli's "circle of constitutions."

reef of destruction, / exhausted by the long lapse of time," *De rerum natura* 2, vv. 1173–74).

Certain end does not mean that it is pointless to pay close attention to how republics perish. Even in this case, for Machiavelli knowledge of the past helps politicians to prevent, at least partly, future dangers. Unlike ancient and humanist thinkers, who had always pointed to the people as the main threat to freedom, the *Discourses* place the responsibility principally on the aristocrats, dismissing the traditional (pro-oligarchic) accusations against the presumed incompetence and unruliness of the masses. In fact, in Machiavelli's view, those who seek to subvert republican institutions and seize absolute power always come from the wealthiest families—even if sometimes these tyrants-to-be cunningly win the support of the people by presenting themselves as its defenders against the rest of the aristocracy. In Rome, with Sulla and Julius Caesar, things followed precisely this course. But, in Florence, the story of the Medicis' victory over the Albizzi and the Strozzi taught a similar lesson.

According to the majority of ancient sources and to all the humanists, the Roman republic collapsed because of three factors: (1) the social unrest that had accompanied the city from its founding, eventually resulting in the self-destructing civil wars of the first century BCE; (2) the malfunctioning of the dictatorship, which facilitated Sulla's and Julius Caesar's rise to absolute power; and (3) the degeneration of mores that was caused by the infectious spread of luxury after the conquest of Greece and the discovery of Eastern indulgences during the second century BCE—as Petrarch wrote, "wealth conquered Rome, once the conqueror of nations" (*Familiares* 11.16.23). As a matter of fact, although some Florentine humanists like Bruni (in the dedication letter of his Latin translation of the *Economics* wrongly attributed to Aristotle, 1420), Bracciolini (*De avaritia*, 1428–1429), and Leon Battista Alberti (*On Family*, 1432–1434) occasionally admitted that the desire for worldly goods could be a positive incentive to human creativity (against medieval ascetic ideals), fifteenth-century authors nevertheless considered extravagance a major threat for the republics and constantly evoked Roman history as the best proof of the evils of lavishness and excessive display. Such an idea was truly contested only by eighteenth-century philosophers and economists like Bernard de Mandeville, David Hume, or Adam Smith, who for the first time asserted that private interest and even some private vices like greed might be the engine of progress and promote public virtues.

As we have seen, Machiavelli openly rejects the first two explanations of the humanists (regarding dictatorship, he recalls in *Discourses* 1.34 that "it is forces that easily acquire names, not names forces"), but the third one is not accepted either. In their place, the *Discourses* offer two alternative elucidations, which connect domestic and foreign factors with great perspicacity. Machiavelli acknowledges that the origin of the long crisis that culminated in Caesar's victory over Pompey in 45 BCE must be sought in the previous century, yet he is not satisfied with the humanists' idea that the cause of the decline was the influx of opulence from the Orient—even if he too believes that, in order to remain free, "well-ordered republics must keep the public rich and the citizens poor" (1.37) and that "poverty bears much better fruits than affluence does" in the republics (3.25). Customs did not change just because voluptuary goods suddenly became available but because at a certain point Rome's ruling class found itself in a novel situation. As the first-century-BCE historian Sallust had noted, as long as the threat from Carthage had lasted, the patricians had remained virtuous and temperate, but when Carthage was defeated, the wealthy became concerned only with increasing their own worth, and they started treating the plebeians ever more harshly than in the past, thereby causing the mass impoverishment that prompted the Gracchi to put forward their land-redistribution proposal (*Bellum Iugurthinum* 41).

Sallust's theory of *metus hostilis* ("fear of the enemy") was obviously known to the humanists, but they generally avoided repeating it, largely because they had understood that it could be used to deny the Romans' merit with the argument that to behave virtuously only out of fear of a foreign menace is not true virtue (as the fifth-century father of the church Augustine had asserted, particularly in *De civitate Dei* 5.12–14). Quite the opposite, Machiavelli has no problem affirming the moralizing power of fear, which in his view is indeed the best tool to control antisocial desires—as already seen, first and foremost in the form of repressive laws (but also a letter by Vettori to Machiavelli dated August 5, 1526, is worth remembering: "I have heard you say on several occasions that fear is the greatest master there is"). During the struggle with Carthage, the Roman ruling class was a model of self-discipline; nevertheless, as soon as Rome subjugated its last competitor in the Mediterranean, its elites abandoned all restraint, and corruption ran rampant at every level of Roman administration, for, instead of picking the best citizens for the offices, as in the past, those who were most ready to favor their clients and supporters gained increasing influence (*Discourses* 1.18 and 3.16). As a consequence of the patricians' unbridled voracity, more and more ordinary citizens fell into poverty, and the Gracchi's abortive attempt to fix the problem of increasing social inequality only hastened the crisis (1.37). The general lesson of the Roman oligarchy's sudden transformation, however, was once again the same: in the absence of appropriate threats (either internal or external), no amount of pedagogy can stop such limitless appetites as greed and luxury.

(It is noteworthy that Machiavelli shows a similar attitude toward the dangers of social conflicts and of excessive wealth. Instead of trying to eradicate them, in both cases he suggests that wise republics should instead carefully control them and turn them into an element of strength. In this regard the opening of the *Discourses*, where in 1.1 Machiavelli attacks his contemporaries' belief that virtue could be attained solely through poverty, is most telling: the wise Romulus chose for his city-to-be a highly fertile area because he knew that without economic resources it is impossible to build a truly powerful state, but at the same time he took precautions against the potentially detrimental effects of wealth on his citizens' customs—and, by doing so, he achieved two apparently incompatible goals at the same time.)

The second explanation for the collapse of the republic calls into question what Machiavelli labels "the prolongation of offices" (3.24). As long as Rome fought in Italy, its peasant soldiers easily alternated between cultivating their own properties and fighting on the battlefield for their city. Yet when the republic found itself cast over larger spaces, and when military campaigns began to last longer (sometimes for several years), the citizens engaged in the wars became increasingly professional soldiers who, victory after victory, felt bound to their generals more than they were to their annually elected magistrates (a perfect example of bad political ties). After the Senate illegally crushed the Gracchi, the rules of political competition changed for good: the spirit of factiousness took over, and both coalitions stopped trusting in the electoral process and in the traditional institutions where for centuries their differences had been resolved more or less peacefully. All parties realized that it was now necessary to rely on military force to prevail, and, in this new context, the generals became the essential pivot of the conflict between the oligarchic and the popular factions, dragging Rome into a terrible sequence of civil wars. After Marius versus Sulla, it was the turn of Julius Caesar versus Pompey and finally of Octavian versus Mark Antony. But in the end, after almost a century of slaughter, servitude under an emperor was the only possible outcome, and on January 16, 27 BCE, the sole winner Octavian took the hallowed name of Augustus.

Roman liberty came to a close that day. Through the combined effect of the ambitious generals' unchecked (and glaringly unconstitutional) power and the fact that there were no more external enemies to fear, even the greatest republic ever seen on earth had entered an irreversible crisis after three and a half centuries of relatively steady government—from 494–490 BCE (when the tribunate of the plebs was first implemented and Rome became a mixed constitution) to 146 BCE (when Carthage was destroyed)—and ultimately died. A dire lesson, but a lesson that, for Machiavelli, should be carefully pondered by every free state before it is too late.

Civic Religion: The Ancients and the Moderns

All things considered, religion plays a modest role in *The Prince*—if we keep in mind that the tract is dedicated to the pope's nephew. In chapter 6 Savonarola is presented as an "unarmed prophet" who did not fully heed the lessons of the founders of states (such as Moses) and who failed to provide himself with the instruments necessary for "holding onto those who had believed" and "to make the non-believers believe"; chapter 11 is dedicated to celebrating the power of the Papal States, which in Machiavelli's mind should support Lorenzo's enterprises; in chapter 13 the duel of David and Goliath offers the cue for an allegory about "one's own armies"; chapters 18 and 20 present religion as one of the most effective foxlike tools to mask the leonine violence of the warring princes (as in the case of Ferdinand of Aragon, who cunningly used it to secure his power against the Spanish feudal aristocracy); the final exhortation to free Italy from the barbarians in chapter 26 is full of references to the Bible, as befits a work addressed to a young man on the verge of becoming the commander of the Papal troops. That's it.

The *Discourses*, on the other hand, require readers to weigh Machiavelli's ideas on religious phenomena and on the role of the papacy in Italian history, if only because of the importance that they would play in his fierce condemnation by the church (and, later, in nineteenth-century celebrations of him as a precursor to the division between religious and lay powers). Machiavelli moves from the bitter consideration that Christianity, for all its emphasis on the afterlife and its rebuke of worldly glory, has made men less inclined to great deeds; hence, "to go to

heaven," most believers "prefer enduring the assaults than aveng-
ing them," and, for this reason, the world had become "prey to
wicked men" (*Discourses* 2.2). With their spectacular bloody sacrifices and emphasis on the active life, pagan cults were completely different, and, because of the importance of the topic (to
which Biondo had dedicated books 1–2 of *Roma triumphans*), a
detailed analysis of the relationships between politics and religion in ancient Rome lies right at the beginning of Machiavelli's commentary (*Discourses* 1.11–15).

Machiavelli ascribes two major political functions to Roman
religion. First, as shown by Numa Pompilius, the second king
of Rome (who was famous for attributing all his most important decisions to his nightly conversations with the nymph
Egeria), the ancients were very skilled in exploiting the people's
credulity to induce them to perform (or not perform) certain
actions according to the needs of the republic (1.11 and 1.13). The
humanists had already taken up this idea (which, by the way, is
enunciated in Scala's *De legibus et iudiciis* precisely via the character of Bernardo Machiavelli), but they had often used it to
argue that the people is incapable of forming sound judgments,
repeating over and over that the masses have to be led by deceit
because they are incapable of grasping what is good and what is
evil for the state. In reaction, Machiavelli tirelessly defends the
intelligence (*Discourses* 1.58) and morality (1.59) of the multitude,
and although he also distinguishes between the people's talent
in picking the right candidates and its lesser ability to deal with
complex questions (1.47), in his view such difference offers no
sufficient motive to leave the republic's government in the hands
of the elite. He thereby presents religion as a powerful remedy
to the assembly's reduced capacity for abstract reasoning—a

remedy that should help the commoners deliberate on difficult issues without depriving them of their political rights. In short, well-meaning deception in the interest of the entire community (and not just of the most powerful families) amounts to nothing more than one of the many emergency measures dear to Machiavelli.

The *Discourses'* most original proposition about religion concerns its ability to force men to behave soundly (1.11 and 1.15). Thanks to the fear of divine punishment, oaths become more solid, and society, which is always threatened by the conduct of egoistic fellow citizens who respect the rules in public but violate them as soon as no one is watching (a distinction that the sophist Glaucon theorizes in book 2 of Plato's *Republic*), is protected from its own members' potential acts of betrayal. Somehow, in Machiavelli, religious faith represents, then, a sort of superbond or metabond that drives men to cooperate in view of a common goal—and in some cases even *against* their (immediate) individual interests. From this point of view, fear of God should be counted as a further component of the *Discourses'* reflection on the bonding ties of politics.

Within this framework Machiavelli inevitably returns to the example of Savonarola. The preacher's impressive rise and equally spectacular fall confirmed to Machiavelli that the age of superstition had not yet passed, as Savonarola had succeeded in convincing a considerable number of his supporters that he possessed the gift of prophecy: "Florentine people do not think that they are either ignorant or uncouth, nevertheless they were persuaded by friar Girolamo Savonarola that he spoke with God" (*Discourses* 1.11). This consideration drives Machiavelli to offer a more positive evaluation of the religious reformer than the one we read in *The Prince*—so much so that in *Discourses* 3.30 he excuses him at least partially for having been an "unarmed prophet" by saying that Savonarola, in fact, understood that it was necessary to imitate Moses, arming himself against his adversaries, but his followers foolishly ignored his warnings.

Faced with a general political crisis, many of Machiavelli's contemporaries had begun to see in the Church of Rome the last bastion of fifteenth-century Italy's blossoming. As with humanistic culture (the other source of pride for the Italians that had not been immediately affected by the upheavals that began in 1494), so too in this case Machiavelli polemically overturns common opinion, blaming the papacy for recent and present defeats. Too weak to unify Italy but strong enough to stop any other regional power from doing so, the pontiffs condemned the peninsula to perpetual division, making it easy prey for France and Spain. Above all, however, with their manifestly immoral behavior, the popes roused religious unbelief in the people and corrupted those regions in particular that were most exposed to the influence of the Roman Curia, starting with Italy (1.12).

Recent defeats are also the result of this crisis. In the future, then, anyone who tries to establish a new republic will inevitably have to enact religious reform too. Nonetheless, Machiavelli has few illusions about the scale of such a challenge: he duly notes that skilled lawgivers are in the same position as artists, who more easily give form to a block of marble that is still intact than to one that has already been partially worked by an inept sculptor—like in this case. With regret, therefore, Machiavelli is forced to admit that the future looks bleak for the Italians. No return to the "first principles" is immediately foreseeable here—and this could be a very bad omen also for the political reforms that Machiavelli would like to implement in Florence in imitation of the Romans. Was it just too late?

How Republics Survive

As already seen, while books 1 and 2 focus on the actions "operated . . . by public counsel" either inside or outside the city (that is, on domestic and foreign policy, respectively), book 3 is devoted to those "operated . . . by private counsel" (*Discourses* 1.1). In this case, though, the organization of the various topics seems less consistent, for Machiavelli deals with several different issues without an apparent unitary line of thought (often reworking ideas that were already present in *The Prince*). As a result, with the exception of a handful of chapters (like 3.1, on the necessity to return periodically to the "first principles"), readers largely neglect this last book. However, Machiavelli's analysis of Rome's political success cannot be properly understood without paying due attention to this section as well.

As a matter of fact, book 3 is for the most part a treatise on republican leadership (and this is probably why there is so much overlap with *The Prince*). Compared to the previous sections, it centers much more on individual figures, with a particularly clear shift in the way warfare is addressed, for here Machiavelli leaves out the shared political and military wisdom of the Romans to dwell on the role that the decisions taken by the single generals (often called "princes" in the republican meaning of "elected high officers") played on the battlefield. In the *Discourses*, even after the best institutions are established and the foundations are laid, individuals can still make a difference—for better or worse. As the first-century BCE Roman poet Horace asked: "What use are empty laws without good mores?" (*Odes* 3.24, vv. 35–36). Therefore, in order to prosper, republics need men of exceptional valor (both from the "mighty" and from the commoners), and to this end they must promote virtue among the citizens through competition for glory, something that princes generally avoid doing. It is a message that the audience in the Rucellai Gardens could only appreciate, but this is not surprising given that in the *Discourses* Machiavelli was especially eager to win the support of his new friends for his neo-Roman project, which he attempted also by showing that there was room for them too in his pro-popular "mixed government."

On the other hand, however, in book 3 Machiavelli repeatedly warns his readers that these same prominent men are too often unwilling to submit to the laws like normal citizens do precisely because of their uncommon features: they tend to be obsessed with personal honor (and, if they come from the elite, with family prestige), to the point that the very qualities for which they are so prized easily turn out to be a potential threat to the cities that do not put appropriate brakes on their aspirations. Somehow, they represent a permanent menace—even if republics cannot do without them. In Machiavelli's view, reconciling outstanding virtue and compliance to the rules becomes, therefore, one of the first imperatives for every free state, no exceptions admitted (including the young aristocrats from the Rucellai Gardens).

Several examples of dangerous ambition already appear in book 1, where much room is given to the tyrannical attempts to overturn the republic made by, for example, the patricians

Marcus Manlius Capitolinus (1.8 and 1.58) and Appius Claudius Crassus (1.35 and 1.40–42). In book 3 Machiavelli returns to the issue, but, rather than expanding on the direct attacks against republican institutions (as in 3.28), he focuses instead on the tensions that inevitably arise between the most prominent citizens' thirst for recognition and the entire community (a topic that was already partially anticipated in the chapters devoted to the risks of ingratitude in 1.28–30) or on the competition for renown among the elite itself. In various forms, while discussing a number of disparate topics, much of book 3 revolves around these two problems, as is clear from the chapters on the bad outcomes of competing commanders (3.15), the danger of the decisions that are made recklessly to redeem a previous failure (3.17), the need for the officers to free themselves of envy in order to benefit their country (3.30), the virtuous actions that earn public figures the support of the people (3.34), the importance of family traditions (3.46), the need to put aside the offenses received as private citizens "for love of the country" (3.47), and so on. Machiavelli thereby induces his readers to consider the pride and the qualities of the citizens of superior distinction as an element of strength of the republic, which must be checked and even tamed but not removed, following what seems like recurring advice in the *Discourses*—as he suggests the same for social conflicts and excessive wealth.

Virtuous people can damage their country against their will, as good intentions often produce effects opposite to the desired outcome. The most extreme cases of hazardous individual political initiative are conspiracies, toward which Machiavelli urges the utmost caution: "for, in the majority of the cases, he who behaves differently ruins himself and his own country"

(3.6—even if in 3.2–5 he praises Lucius Iunius Brutus's shrewdness in the ousting of Tarquin the Proud). In previous decades, leading humanists had devoted some historiographical tracts to the most spectacular fifteenth-century conspiracies (Alberti, *Porcaria coniuratio*, 1453; Poliziano, *Coniurationis commentarium*, 1478; Pontano, *De bello Neapolitano*, posthumously printed in 1509); nevertheless, no one had ever subjected such plots to theoretical analysis before Machiavelli, who had already applied himself to this topic in chapter 19 of *The Prince* (a chapter that was inspired by the reading of the Greek historian Herodian in Poliziano's Latin translation and that was dedicated to dissecting the ill-fated deaths of second-century Roman emperors). The longest chapter of the *Discourses* stems from this interest in the way plots are organized (and in why they fail so often); however, here the same events are observed as much from the point of view of the schemers as from that of the princes under attack, in an incredibly elaborate chain of hypotheses and counterhypotheses with no equivalent in the whole of Machiavelli's work.

As already seen in *The Prince*, for Machiavelli excellence has a lot to do with the ability to cope with the unforeseen and to manage flux. The concluding chapter of the *Discourses*, entitled "To keep a republic free, it needs new provisions every day" (3.49), is particularly significant in this respect. Compared with *The Prince*'s exhortation to free Italy from the barbarians, this seems to be a finale in a minor key, where many creative remedies devised by the Romans to deal with unexpected crises are quickly reviewed one after the other, out of chronological order: the Senate's timely response against the murderous plot of more than 170 Roman matrons to poison their husbands (331 BCE), the suppression of the so-called Bacchanalia conspiracy while Rome was engaged in a challenging war against Macedonia (186 BCE), the exemplary punishment reserved for the few Roman soldiers who survived the defeat at Cannae (216 BCE), and the reform of Roman tribes set up by Quintus Fabius Maximus in order to prevent newcomers from corrupting ancient mores (303 BCE). Indeed, even if the examples chosen are deliberately very different from one another and seem completely disconnected, they all refer to one and the same virtue: the Romans' extraordinary ability to consistently come up with novel measures—which is what really interests Machiavelli here.

This is a vital point. The *Discourses* opens under the banner of imitation of the ancients; nevertheless, for Machiavelli such apprenticeship is not enough. Since history never repeats itself in a perfectly identical manner, no republic can ever preserve its freedom only by following the great lessons of the past—not even the lesson of Rome. For this reason, nothing is further from the *Discourses*' spirit than the fetishism of Romulus's original constitution and even of later "mixed government." To use the rhetorical categories dear to the humanists, at a certain point the moment of "imitation" (*imitatio*), in which the moderns scrupulously follow the teachings of the most renowned classics, must be supplanted by the moment of "emulation" (*aemulatio*), when those who come after have so thoroughly internalized the ancients' wisdom that they can aspire to equate and surpass them by taking an original path. Without a special taste for experimentation and the ability to adapt to new times—Machiavelli warns at the end of the *Discourses*—even the best institutions do not guarantee by themselves the success of the republic. However glorious, the examples of the ancients must respond to an ever-changing present that requires unremitting imagination—both from the "mighty" and from the commoners. The Romans never failed to do so. And it is precisely on this impassioned tribute to Rome's political creativity that the *Discourses* take leave from their readers.

4

Comeback Kid

His Holiness [Giulio de' Medici, now Clement VII]
replied: "Tell him [Machiavelli] to come, I'm very
glad of it."

—Francesco Guicciardini to Niccolò Machiavelli,
November 12, 1526

Politics, Again

Like many of his contemporaries, Machiavelli was inclined to associate human instability with the medieval image of Fortune's wheel and its whimsical turns. For a man at the peak of success, the wheel signaled the bad luck that would sooner or later knock him down, while, to all those who were momentarily at a low point, it promised imminent redemption. During Machiavelli's youth, however, an alternative classical iconography began to emerge in Florence. Because it was perceived as signifying an overly mechanical alternation of good and bad cycles, the wheel disappeared from view; Fortune was now represented as a naked young woman with attractive features, on a ship, sometimes in the company of a dolphin (a benign symbol of speed and versatility). Above all, this new image of Fortune took on the distinctive feature of the iconography of another goddess linked to time, Occasion: a long lock of hair hanging on the forehead, which, along with a completely bare nape of the neck, was meant to signify that opportunities are offered only briefly and should be taken immediately, before Fortune turns her back on you. Machiavelli seems to have learned this lesson after the disaster of 1512, when he tried in every way to overcome the opposition he had faced after the fall of the republic. It took years, but in the end, thanks to his friends from the Rucellai Gardens and his determination, he succeeded in at least partly getting back into the political game.

Contrary to the nineteenth-century Romantic mythology about him, in the last part of his life Machiavelli hardly lacked public recognition, both as a man of letters and as a renowned adviser in political and military matters. Already in 1516–1517 he had been asked by Paolo Vettori (the brother of his friend Francesco) to assist him in setting up a fleet to fight the Saracen pirates (by mandate of the pope), and then between 1521 and 1522 Machiavelli was repeatedly consulted about a potential reform of Florentine institutions at a time when the Medici felt particularly vulnerable, not least because their hold on the city had already been rendered more precarious by the premature deaths of the youngest members of the family, Giuliano (1516) and Lorenzo (1519), and then of Leo X in 1521. It is significant that, in the brief but dense *Discursus Florentinarum rerum* that he composed in 1521 at the request of Cardinal Giulio de Medici, Machiavelli stood by his old position: to win the favor of the people there was no alternative but to reopen the Great Council.

A man of his experience could be useful, especially in times of war, and Italy was not lacking military conflicts. After a short pause, the struggle for control of the peninsula was revived by the competition between two very young kings: Francis I of France (born in 1494) and Charles I of Spain (born in 1500), who in 1519 was also elected Holy Roman Emperor as Charles V and suddenly found himself ruling over half of Europe (the Iberian peninsula, the Kingdom of Naples, Austria, Flanders, and Germany), as well as over the newly conquered territories in the Americas, which were rich in precious metals. As a result of the new wars, in 1522 France definitively lost the Duchy of Milan (which it had reconquered in 1515), and Francis I was even taken prisoner in the disastrous battle of Pavia against the Spaniards (February 24, 1525). Faced with this sensational imbalance of forces, in 1526 the new pope, Clement VII (born Giulio de' Medici and elected to the papacy in 1523), decided to deploy Florence and the Papal States alongside France and Venice in the League of Cognac against Charles V in an attempt to find a new equilibrium. For Machiavelli it was the final opportunity to take part in big politics by carrying out various logistical tasks for his friend Guicciardini, whom the pope had chosen as general lieutenant of the Florentine and Papal army. Even if these assignments were not as important as those he had fulfilled under Soderini, Machiavelli can hardly be viewed as a political outcast in this late phase of his life.

The legend of an ostracized Machiavelli rests largely on a final disappointment. In the context of the war between Charles V and Clement VII, on May 6, 1527, imperial troops set about sacking Rome, and the pontiff had to shut himself up in the Castel Sant'Angelo fortress to escape his enemies. About ten days later, on May 17, the Florentine people took advantage of the opportunity to rise up against the Medici and restore the republic, including the Great Council (while the oligarchic Council of Seventy was immediately abolished). This was what Machiavelli had long hoped for: a sort of unexpected return to his youth. So, when the Great Council decided to hold a vote for a new secretary of the chancery, Machiavelli applied for the post. Unfortunately for him, the current secretary, Francesco Tarugi, was reelected by the assembly on June 10, probably because of the hostility of the still-influential Savonarola faction toward Machiavelli. On this occasion, however, there was no time for a rematch with Fortune: exactly ten days later, Machiavelli died suddenly at fifty-eight—in the sixteenth century not at all an insignificant age. The wheel had made its final turn for him.

Florence on the Stage: *The Mandrake*

The last part of Machiavelli's life was particularly rich in literary projects. Of his youthful works, only one had circulated in print (in 1506): the *Decennale*, a text of 550 verses in *terza rima* (like Dante's *Commedia*), in which he recounted the ten years from 1494 to 1504, not least to promote his own militia project. A decade later, when he discovered that Ludovico Ariosto had failed to mention him in a list of contemporary writers in his great epic poem the *Orlando furioso* (1516), he wrote to his friend Lodovico Alamanni, who at that time, like Ariosto, was in Rome: "I read the *Orlando furioso* . . . and the whole poem is truly beautiful, and in many places admirable. If you meet him, recommend me to him, and tell him that I only regret that, having mentioned so many poets, he left me out like a cock" (December 17, 1517).

Among his most important works worthy of mention are the unfinished poem *The Golden Ass*, inspired by Apuleius's second-century Latin novel and about a thousand verses long; two short novellas, *Belfagor Archdemon*, inspired by the fifteenth-century French chronicler Jean Le Fèvre's *Lamentations of Matthew*, and the *Epistle on the Plague*, the latter erroneously long attributed to Machiavelli's friend Lorenzo Strozzi; and the *Discourse on Our Language*, conceived to refute those who, in the wake of Pietro Bembo's *Discourses of the Vulgar Language* (1525), believed that contemporary writers should employ only the vocabulary and the syntax of the fourteenth-century great Tuscan classics (Boccaccio's tales from the *Decameron* for prose and Petrarch's sonnets and songs from the *Canzoniere* for poetry) and that expressions used in modern spoken Florentine were to be steadfastly avoided. However, Machiavelli distinguished himself above all in the theater, thanks to a comedy that remains one of the most canonical plays of the Italian repertory: *The Mandrake*, which was first staged in Florence and then in Rome in 1520, probably before Pope Leo X.

Since the end of the fifteenth century Roman comedies had enjoyed a true golden age, when many productions of the ancient plays by Plautus and Terence were staged in vernacular translation in the courts of Ferrara and Mantua (though in Rome, Bologna, and Florence the shows were still performed in Latin). Hence, by the 1510s the production of Italian comedies written in imitation of classical ones had become very fashionable in the peninsula. The young Machiavelli fully shared this enthusiasm for ancient theater. He transcribed Terence's *Eunuchus* and translated Terence's *Andria* into Italian, and another of his later comedies, *Clizia* (first staged in 1525 with musical intermezzos by the famous French composer Philippe Verdelot), was a rewriting of Plautus's *Casina*. It is not surprising, therefore, that the scenario of *The Mandrake* was also inspired by Latin comedies, in which it almost invariably happens that a young man fights with an old(er) one for the love of a young girl to marry (or to keep as an attractive slave), until the former manages to prevail thanks to the help of an ingenious servant. Yet no less evident in *The Mandrake* is the influence of Boccaccio and of the many short stories of the Tuscan narrative tradition, where the plot often turns on an adulterous couple's efforts to meet behind a jealous husband's back.

Apart from these unmistakable sources of inspiration, the comedy is an original work, one as valuable as the masterpieces of the ancients, according to a strict judge like Voltaire, who wrote, "Machiavelli's *The Mandrake* alone is perhaps worth more than all the comedies of Aristophanes" (*An Essay on Universal History*, 1756). The greatest strength of the play is its perfect plot, devoid of the mechanical procedures that Roman comedy profusely deployed to add dynamism to the story at the expense of verisimilitude (sudden arrivals, unpredictable recognitions, pairs of twins mistaken for each other, etc.). In love with the beautiful and virtuous Lucrezia, the wife of the old and naive Nicia Calfucci, the young Callimaco Guadagni devises an elaborate plan to seduce her with the help of his cunning servant Ligurio. Since the couple is unable to have children, Callimaco pretends to be a doctor who knows how to make Lucrezia pregnant: all it will take, he says, is that she drink a potion of mandrake, an herb with magical powers. There is only one drawback: after such therapy, the first man to sleep with Lucrezia will die from the mandrake's poison. Ligurio, however, has a solution for this inconvenience, too, and he persuades Nicia to trick a humble servant into Lucrezia's bed. Naturally, the servant will be none other than Callimaco in disguise. Thanks to the help of a corrupt friar, Timoteo, even Lucrezia is convinced with arguments taken from Renaissance casuistry (case-based moral theology devoted to resolving problematic ethical questions) that it is not a sin to let a man die so that she may give birth to a son. The plan is fulfilled, and the two young people spend that night together, and many more in the future.

Although *The Mandrake* was subjected to some rather coarse allegorical readings during the twentieth century (Callimaco as a symbol of the Medici, who conquer Lucrezia-Florence with the help of the church by stealing her from the old republican elites, embodied by Nicia), the play owes its strength to Machiavelli's ability at least partly to eschew the fixed recurring types of Latin theater in favor of a livelier cast of personae, who are described in terms not only of their external comic appearance but also of their secret motivations (for this reason, in his 1787 *Memories*, the great eighteenth-century Italian playwright Carlo Goldoni welcomed *The Mandrake* as the first "comedy of characters" ever written). The audience immediately feels that *The Mandrake* took inspiration also from real life and not just from its ancient sources, and it is here, in his study of Florentine individuals, with their weaknesses and their obsessions, that Machiavelli demonstrates his superior knowledge of the world. Moreover, a similar quest for realism is visible in the precise chronology of the plot (Callimaco was born in 1474 and moved to Paris after his parents' death in 1484 but could not come back to Florence in 1494, as planned, because of Charles VIII's invasion, and did so only in 1504, when the action is set) and in the many Florentine locations mentioned in the play (the Old and the New Markets, the Spini and the Proconsolo Benches, the Loggia Tornaquinci, the "Street of Love," etc.).

This adherence to Florence's everyday life does not, of course, preclude *The Mandrake* from having a political subtext. For example, Nicia is a walking caricature of the false wisdom of old age, and his name is probably derived from the aristocratic Athenian political leader Nicias, who after many hesitations led his city to a devastating military defeat in Sicily (an allusion to the foolish caution and incompetence of the Florentine oligarchs whom Machiavelli detested). More generally, *The Mandrake* can be read as yet another Machiavellian celebration of the rare virtuous individual capable of going beyond appearances and mastering the unpredictable flow of events—just like Callimaco does.

Two other characters deserve attention. Friar Timoteo (whose commentary closes the play) is a descendant of the *Decameron*'s many corrupt clergymen, and he has often drawn the attention of readers who are attuned to the work's political subtext. For instance, he comically repeats the opinion that Machiavelli had formulated in chapter 8 of *The Prince* about the possibility of finding a "remedy" with God for the wicked actions that benefit the entire community: "The clemency of God is great: if a man does not lack the will, he never lacks the time to repent." Moreover, in light of Machiavelli's teaching about political ties and links, it is no small matter that Timoteo alone has the power to dissolve one bond (marriage) in order to allow Callimaco to forge another. The fact that it is a man of God who helps profane the sacrament of matrimony naturally played a decisive role in fueling the comedy's reputation for immorality. Even if it seems strange, this element of the story is not at odds with reports of a staging at Leo X's court. Before the Council of Trent (1545–1563), the Catholic Church was in fact very tolerant on these matters: it was still possible to laugh lightheartedly at an ending such as this, in which Nicia, Lucrezia, and Callimaco assume positions resembling Renaissance pictorial representations of the marriage of the Virgin (as in Pietro Perugino or Raphael), so that the two lovers celebrate in the church a mock wedding in front of the cuckolded husband—a desecration of the sacrament that would appear intolerably blasphemous just a few decades later. As a result, *The Mandrake* would enter permanently into the repertories of Italian stage companies only after the abolition of theater censorship in 1962.

Lucrezia is a central character too. Machiavelli's contemporaries could not help but associate her with the virtuous Roman matron Lucretia, who was raped by Tarquin the Proud's son and thereafter committed suicide because of the dishonor, provoking the expulsion of the kings. Already Enea Silvio Piccolomini, the future Pope Pius II, had played on the comic contrast when he gave the same name to the unfaithful wife at the center of a seduction plot in his *Historia de duobus amantibus* (1444, first printed in 1467), one of fifteenth-century Europe's unrivaled bestsellers. In Machiavelli, though, the choice of name is no longer just the pretext for an easy laugh, as the lesson of *The Mandrake* is hardly that all women, even the most virtuous, eventually succumb to the wants of the flesh (this according to an old misogynist tradition); rather, the play teaches that true virtue does not always require the Roman Lucretia's valiant intransigence and that, in particular situations, a more accommodating approach may be acceptable and even preferable (although this malleability clearly does not belittle the value of Lucretia's exemplary sacrifice in the context of Rome's transition from tyranny to republican freedom). Since her adulterous relationship remains secret, the Florentine Lucrezia's honor will be preserved; in addition, by agreeing to keep Callimaco as a lover, the woman will also delight in a long-awaited child, an honorable partner, and, on the day old Nicia dies, a new legitimate husband who boasts all the qualities that the first one signally lacked. In short, a utilitarian ethic triumphs, where religious imperatives have no importance, honor is reduced to a question of perspective, and the result counts more than anything else. For, in the last scene of the play, set in a church (probably Santa Maria Novella), everyone is happy and content, especially the deceived Nicia, who, grateful for the help he has received, already savors his belated and much-desired fatherhood. All's well that ends well—as Machiavelli, himself the son of an illegitimate child, had no problem recognizing.

The Invention of Tactics: *The Art of War*

For Machiavelli, war is the moment of truth, the test for which every prince and every republic must be prepared even in times of peace. It is not difficult to recognize in his pages the scars of Italy's most recent history, when, since 1494, the peninsula had been relentlessly pillaged by the great European powers. Furthermore, it was a period of profound changes in combat strategy and tactics. In comparison with fifteenth-century warfare, in which military campaigns consisted of a series of exhausting sieges, the unprecedented recourse to increasingly lethal artillery had redressed the balance in favor of the offensive, rendering completely useless the strongholds that lacked the most modern defensive structures of the so-called bastion fort, or trace italienne (first introduced in the 1480s), and pushing those under attack to face their enemies in the open field instead. Such a transformation, however, required a complete rethinking of how warfare should be conducted, and Machiavelli, who had accumulated considerable practical experience working on the militia project, did not shy away from such a challenge in the subsequent years.

While *The Prince* teaches that "virtue" is practically synonymous with "one's own armies" and in the last chapter announces a reform of the infantry that would make it unbeatable against any enemy (without going into detail), the *Discourses* probe the issue further, devoting the whole of book 2 to Roman war techniques. In addition to analyzing how the Romans forged alliances, occupied enemy lands, and gradually integrated defeated populations into their own (*Discourses* 2.3–4, 2.6–7, 2.21), Machiavelli addresses many other particular issues and especially the need to avoid overreliance on wealth (2.10), artillery (2.17), and fortresses (2.24), a topic that had been already discussed in the twentieth chapter of *The Prince*; moreover, special attention is also given to the superiority of infantry over cavalry (*Discourses* 2.18)—a clear effect of the Swiss pikemen's spectacular successes all over Europe. Even in his commentary on Livy, however, Machiavelli avoids discussing the most technical aspects of warfare, which are at the core of just one writing: *The Art of War*, his only major political text that circulated in print during his life (Giunti, 1521, with a dedication to Lorenzo Strozzi).

The Art of War is in many ways a peculiar book. On the one hand, it is an extremely specialized treatise discussing very detailed questions, such as the materials and workmanship of various weapons—and this explains why it is by far Machiavelli's least-read major work today. On the other hand, it is also the writing to which Machiavelli clearly devoted the most care in terms of literary refinement, from the elegant syntax (so different from *The Prince*'s contracted and, at times, difficult prose) to the unprecedented choice of the dialogue form to express his ideas: a decision that made *The Art of War* the very first military dialogue in Western literature.

The imaginary discussion takes place in the Rucellai Gardens in September 1516, when an important visit offers the starting point: the arrival in Florence of Fabrizio Colonna, an elderly condottiere from the powerful Roman family who in previous years had served under Charles VIII, the Aragonese of Naples, and then the Spaniards. The old soldier senses that his end is approaching, but, although he is no longer in a position single-handedly to remedy the faults of the mercenary system that had made his fortune, he is nonetheless confident that his experience could at least benefit the new generation (as he says, with a memorable maxim: in war "the unarmed rich man is the prize of the soldier in need"). For this reason, the young aristocrats who frequent the Rucellai Gardens (Cosimo Rucellai, Zanobi Buondelmonti, Battista della Palla, and Luigi Alamanni) take turns interrogating the aged Fabrizio, thereby giving him the opportunity to formulate in detail his project for a neo-Roman reform of warfare, which in reality is Machiavelli's. From this point of view, *The Art of War* is a perfect example of Renaissance monological and "closed" dialogue, where a single perspective dominates and secondary speakers merely play a minor role, unlike dialogical and "open" dialogues, where, by contrast, more weight is given to alternative viewpoints (also with a greater ambiguity).

Inevitably, issues already addressed in his previous writings return, starting with the heated invective against the Italian princes (and, implicitly, the humanists who taught them) that closes the dialogue:

> Before they tasted the blows of foreign wars, our Italian princes believed that it was enough for a prince to know how to meditate a sharp reply in his office, to write a beautiful letter, to show wit and promptness in his words and sayings, to know how to manage a deceit, to adorn himself with gems and gold, to sleep and eat with greater splendor than the others, to have an abundance of lustful pleasures, to rule the subjects greedily and superbly, to rot in idleness, to give the military command without merit, to scorn anyone who showed them any praiseworthy behavior, to want their words to be listened to as the responses of an oracle; nor did they realize that they were preparing to be prey to whoever would attack them. Hence in 1494 the great terrors, the sudden escapes and the miraculous losses were born; and, therefore, three very powerful states which were in Italy [that is, Naples, Milan, and Venice] were sacked and ruined several times. But what is worse is that those who remained persevere in the same error and live in the same disorder.

In many respects, Machiavelli conceives his new work as a means to clarify his prior military thought—like in the case of the invincible (but mysterious) "third order" that was mentioned in chapter 26 of *The Prince* and now turns out to be just a combination of pikemen and soldiers armed with swords and shields (described in *The Art of War* as, respectively, a new version of the Macedonian phalanx and the Roman legion). What has changed, however, is the overall tone. War now takes center stage, and Machiavelli is no longer afraid to confront even the most complicated questions raised by contemporary combat practices. But this is a big change not just in comparison with *The Prince* and the *Discourses*, because, by discussing any sort of technical problem in depth, Machiavelli intends immediately to distinguish himself also from humanists such as Roberto Valturio (in his *De re militari*, 1455, first printed in 1472) or Biondo (in books 6–7 of his *Roma triumphans*), whose military theory still depended largely on Vegetius's fourth-century *Epitoma rei militaris* and Frontinus's first-century *Strategemata*, the two Roman treatises on warfare most widely read during the Middle Ages.

The *Art of War*'s greatest novelty probably lies in the role that Machiavelli assigns to the tactical dimension, that is, to the deployment and movement of troops (the word "tactic" derives from the Greek verb *tassein*, "to place"). Beyond etymology, however, "tactics" means first of all a different operational scale, one more attentive to how smaller units interact with one another during battle and condition the final outcome of the clash. This alone would be enough to distinguish *The Art of War* from Vegetius and Frontinus as well as from their fifteenth-century imitators, who all acknowledged only the brain of the general (that is, the overall vision of the battlefield) and the brawn of the soldiers, leaving out any intermediate element that could ensure good communication between the two extremes. On the one hand, Vegetius teaches how to choose recruits, how to train them, which offensive and defensive weapons to equip them with, and the means to bolster their morale even in the most difficult moments; on the other hand, on a strategic scale, he centers on the great maneuvers of encirclement and breakthrough or the unconventional moves with which the commander-in-chief can reverse the outcome of a battle. The connection between these two levels of operation remains, however, almost nonexistent, for in his treatise the task of connecting them is entrusted generically to the soldiers' discipline or resolved with a list of names of officers who should ensure—it is not clear exactly how—that at the appropriate time the general's orders reach the soldiers and that those orders are correctly executed. On this topic even less is said in Frontinus's *Strategemata*, where (as suggested by the title) the leader of the army is taught how to plan his own strategy and to anticipate that of the enemy, while the other aspects of combat are completely disregarded.

Everything changes with *The Art of War*. First of all, Machiavelli focuses on a smaller scale, even if he does not forsake a unifying perspective on the battle as a whole nor a detailed description of all the phases of the clash (this comes in book 3, in one of the treatise's most stylistically elaborate passages and a real jewel of Italian prose). The general is always at his post, where he maintains his usual directive function, and so too is the simple soldier. For the first time, however, Machiavelli tackles the problem of how the directives that start from above can reach individual combatants in a timely and unambiguous fashion. To develop the bodily metaphor that is often used in the dialogue to allude to the army as a single aggregate of men, one might say that Machiavelli is primarily interested in the nervous system of his neo-Roman legion and with his work intends to fill an obvious gap in existing military theory.

The Art of War states several times that the ability to maneuver—that is, to implement the instructions coming from above quickly and effectively—is even more important than the soldiers' individual courage and field experience. This is a radical statement and a major change but one that can be easily explained in the context of the military reforms that were undertaken in Italy in the 1490s, when Swiss fighting techniques had begun to spread throughout the peninsula. Large companies of pikemen had proven to be almost unbeatable only if they maintained their formation—and Machiavelli is clearly thinking about the Swiss way of taking up a position before the enemy also when he discusses soldiers armed with swords and shields in the Roman manner. His attention thus shifts from the fighters' generic warlike ardor to their ability to perform movements according to received orders. It is useless to anticipate the enemy's plans, study the battlefield, or devise original stratagems if the army cannot properly execute commands: hence, the recruits must be painstakingly drilled in due time to facilitate such coordinated maneuvers against the enemy.

Many proposals in *The Art of War* stem from this fundamental requirement, beginning with the importance attached to those low-level officers who first have the task of training conscripts and then guiding them in the melee: the so-called *capodieci*. This heir of the Roman decurion is none other than the most experienced soldier, who takes up a position at the end of each line and—as a sort of cornerstone—is called upon to support his infantrymen from the most exposed, and therefore most dangerous, position (the *capodieci* has no companion who, with his shield, could offer even partial protection for the right side of his body). Similarly, the considerable care that Machiavelli gives to the aural and visual signals through which commands are formulated in order to avoid misunderstandings can be traced back to the same concern for a perfect interaction between the different parts of the army. Any uncertainty, any delay, can be fatal once the battle has begun. And it is to prevent such mishaps that the recruits' exercise turns out to be so critically important.

Similar worries probably motivate another of *The Art of War*'s most innovative aspects: the use of a variety of graphics to show as precisely as possible how men should be disposed on the ground in order to cope with the different exigencies of military life (on the march, on the battlefield, in the encampment). On this point, Machiavelli developed the lesson of a lesser-known ancient military treatise included in a 1487 miscellaneous volume in which he probably also read Vegetius and Frontinus: Aelian's *On the Military Arrangements of the Greeks*. This brief Greek tract of the second century, just some thirty pages long in the Latin translation executed a few years earlier by the humanist Theodore Gaza, was destined to enjoy great renown during the sixteenth century; before Machiavelli, however, no one had realized its importance. Instead of concentrating on the strategic dimension (the conduct of an entire campaign or the course of a battle), *On the Military Arrangements of the Greeks* focuses on the movements of single units, with the objective of ensuring the tight coherence of the whole phalanx. It is first of all a question of size: in only one case does Aelian put more than two hundred men at arms in the field, while in most of its charts he does not go beyond a few dozen. Hence, the nickname of "Tactician" (by which the ancients distinguished the author of *On the Military Arrangements of the Greeks* from the second-century Greek historian Claudius Aelianus) turns out to be particularly appropriate in the double meaning of the term—"tactics" as the art of arranging troops but also as the opposite of "strategy" in terms of scale (figure 4.1).

Just as in *The Prince* with Xenophon and Herodian and in the *Discourses* with Polybius and Dionysius, so too in *The Art of War* Machiavelli seems to have been the first to exploit the teachings of a Greek author who had only recently become accessible in the West. Some of his key ideas, such as the attention given to low-level officers, are in fact already present in Aelian and clearly derive from his treatise. But even without discussing in detail the convergences and differences between the two works, it suffices to say that Machiavelli seems to have learned from *On the Military Arrangements of the Greeks* first and foremost a working method that privileged the "microphysics" of war and emphasized primarily the most minuscule aspects of the battle, rather than broader issues like the movements of the whole army (issues that are, nevertheless, addressed whenever necessary). If, according to a maxim attributed to the famous American general Omar Nelson Bradley, "amateurs talk strategy, professionals talk logistics," it is clear that in *The Art of War* Machiavelli intends to speak as the true professional that he was.

The reactions of Machiavelli's contemporaries to the only work he published in print are very telling about the novelty of his approach. *The Art of War* was widely read, immediately plagiarized in Spain, and inspired King Francis I's reform of the French army in 1534. At the same time, however, Machiavelli's

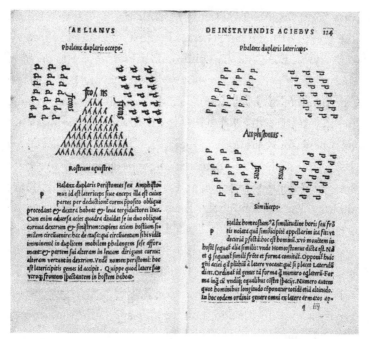

Figure 4.1. The deployment of troops in Aelian's *De instruendis aciebus* (Rome: Eucharius Silber, 1487).

desire to control even the most detailed aspects of the battle was received with suspicion by other readers. The earliest critic was probably the bishop of Agen and famous short-story writer Matteo Bandello, who in one of his novellas derided Machiavelli's inability to put his complex figures and movements into practice when the condottiere Giovanni dalle Bande Nere finally gave him the opportunity to set out real troops in a real drill: "It became clear then how big is the difference between him who knows and has never applied what he knows, and him who— besides the knowledge—gets his hands dirty, as it is customary to say" (*Novels* 1.40, 1554). The anecdote is clearly fictional (and very likely inspired by Cicero's *De oratore* 2.18.76, which tells of the great Carthaginian general Hannibal deriding the second-century-BCE Aristotelian philosopher Phormio, who dared to discuss warfare in his presence without having had any real experience of the battlefield); nonetheless, it is revealing because it indicates the distrust with which Machiavelli's insistence on a new dimension of war—tactics—was viewed. *The Art of War*'s ambition to regulate the slightest aspect of the fight seemed ridiculous to some, and, as another skeptical military theorist, the French scholar Blaise de Vigèneres, would write a few decades later, with all his diagrams and drawings there was the risk of mistaking something as serious as war for the game of chess (*Onasander's Military Art*, posthumously published in 1605). Initially, not everyone was ready to follow Machiavelli's advice. In the end, however, his approach proved to be the right one.

Important thinkers have many good ideas; the few truly great ones have just one or two, but these are decisive and run obsessively through all their works, forever changing the way the most diverse issues are observed afterward. Machiavelli's fundamental intuition is probably that all human congregations can be described in terms of social/institutional/emotional bonds that must be loosened or tightened according to the needs of the moment—and that the outcome of any political project depends mainly on how this delicate operation is done. One could even argue that all the quarrels about the interpretation of Machiavelli's thought have for centuries revolved around how we understand the many ties that we encounter at the heart of his work: Who pulls the strings in the end? The shrewd new prince? The elite? Both the mighty and the people? Its leaders? All of them, depending on the situation? Or rather nobody, because the mixed constitution devised by the wise original lawgiver or improved step by step through social conflict is a perfect mechanism that operates on its own? The army is evidently no exception to this fundamental insight. Quite the contrary, it illustrates Machiavelli's general principle with absolute clarity because it complies even better with a schematic representation than other aspects of collective life.

Machiavelli's attention to military tactics is therefore yet another sign of his fascination with everything that has the power to connect and hold together: fear, love, institutions, religion. It is therefore obvious that, in his view, military theorists who neglect these aspects of warfare deserve no more consideration than philosophers who (like the humanists of his time) spout noble words on the importance of civic virtues yet care insufficiently about the means by which men should be headed—or even forced—to cooperate for the common good. This is the crucial point: in peace as in war, to disregard the connections between the overall aim and the actions of individuals, or between ends and means, is tantamount to imagining "republics and principalities" that nobody has ever "seen or known" (*The Prince* 15). In light of his war theory, one possible definition of Machiavelli's much-celebrated realism could therefore be just this: the ability to reconnect the brain to the arm, that is, to set in motion the most distant peripheries of the political or military organism through an articulated system of nerve branches (to take up the corporeal metaphor again). In this perspective, *The Art of War* repeats the same lesson that, in other fields and contexts, both *The Prince* and the *Discourses* had already tried to teach their readers.

Political Theory by Other Means: *The Florentine Histories*

He who controls the past controls the future. The humanists had their own way of expressing this concept, quoting from Horace on literature's power to render princes and generals immortal: "Many valiant heroes lived before Agamemnon, / but a long night / envelops them, without glory and tears, / because there is no singer to celebrate them" (*Odes* 4.9, vv. 25–28). Such a bold claim was also instrumental to propagandizing their own skills, of course, for the new classicizing authors wrote a Latin almost indistinguishable from that of the ancients, and they knew how to imitate Cicero and Virgil like nobody else before. The humanists' promise of eternity thereby became a strong reason for their success among Italian and European elites.

Political communities were no less attracted to such celebrations, and the first attempts to write a history that followed the conventions of the ancients for the greater glory of a city predictably happened in Florence, then the epicenter of the humanistic movement. Already during the fourteenth century some Florentines had kept a record of the major events of the commune, and, above all, Giovanni Villani's twelve-book *New Chronicles* (covering the period up to 1346) had enjoyed wide recognition among his fellow citizens. However, the new classicizing culture required an updating of Villani's narrative that would apply the principles of humanism to historical writing as well. The difficult task was performed by two of the greatest authors of the time, Leonardo Bruni and Poggio Bracciolini, both originally from Arezzo but destined for spectacular careers between Rome and Florence. In 1416, when he was chancellor of the republic, Bruni dedicated the first book of his *Historiarum*

Florentini populi libri (up to the first half of the thirteenth century) to the ruling magistrates, and his efforts were rewarded with the granting of citizenship; later, when he reached the ninth book, he received a complete exemption from taxes (one of the highest honors to which a Florentine could aspire); then, little by little, the books stretched to twelve in number, covering the events up to 1402. No modern city had ever been celebrated in a fashion that was so close to the ancients, and, when Bruni died in 1444, the republic urged the sculptor Bernardo Rossellino to immortalize the deceased chancellor holding a copy of his history in a monumental sarcophagus that was to be placed in the church of Santa Croce. It is hardly surprising, therefore, that when Bracciolini was appointed secretary of the republic in 1453 he attempted a similar undertaking. However, his turbulent relations with the Medici led him to resign from that prestigious office just a few years later, so his history was never formally offered to the city and remained incomplete (as, in fact, was Bruni's).

Both written in elegant Ciceronian prose, the two works only partially overlapped. While Bruni had followed Livy's model, trying to offer a complete account of the events of Florence from its legendary foundation at Sulla's times, Bracciolini imitated the first-century-BCE historian Sallust, who was universally appreciated for two monographs on (respectively) Rome's second-century-BCE struggle against the African king Jugurtha and Catiline's first-century-BCE conspiracy to overturn the republic. Bracciolini therefore focused on the wars fought by Florence from 1350 to 1455, in particular against the Visconti of Milan. From many other points of view, however, Bruni's and Bracciolini's books are very similar. Both of them carefully selected materials from medieval chronicles, eliminating anything that was improper for political history (information about the climate, miraculous apparitions, assorted anecdotes, etc.); both enriched (and embellished) the narrative with long speeches that were put into the mouths of the main historical figures (as the Greeks and Romans had done, often arranging them in pairs in order to articulate what the different sides were fighting for); both described with true mastery the course of the principal battles. Their greatest achievement, however, was probably the use Bruni and Bracciolini made of classical Latin's optative constructions (those that express wish, hope, desire, fear, etc.) to weigh the potential alternative outcomes of each major event. By recovering this stylistic device, their narratives were turned into extremely sophisticated political analyses that were functional to exploring the "counterfactual conditionals" not less perceptively than Greek and Roman historians had done.

Humanistic historiography may appear superficial and even untruthful by today's standards, particularly because of the freedom with which Bruni, Bracciolini, and their countless followers invented these long speeches instead of adhering closely to the scarce available archival documentation. It would be a mistake, however, to consider such oratorical exercises as forgeries (as has often been the case in the last two hundred years). Fifteenth-century readers were well aware that such addresses were not a faithful transcription of the words actually uttered but rather interpretations of the aims that moved the principal figures of Florentine history; to avoid any possible confusion, on this point in the opening of his *Gesta Ferdinandi regis Aragonum* (1445–1446) the great humanist Lorenzo Valla asked a rhetorical question: "Or is there anyone who believes that those orations we read in the histories [of the ancients] are true and that they were not adapted to the characters, the moment, and the situation by an artist not less eloquent than wise, so that they would teach us how to speak and reason?" By exploiting a literary convention inherited from the ancients, authors could instruct their fellow citizens in the behaviors that had benefited and those that had harmed the motherland, and Bruni and Bracciolini both embraced this opportunity. Thanks to a deeper knowledge of their past, the Florentines, they hoped, would act more wisely in the future.

Bruni's and Bracciolini's narratives were enthusiastically received and, after their translations into Italian were printed together in 1476, they achieved the rank of a semiofficial history of their city. For this reason, a few years later, another illustrious secretary of the chancery, Bartolomeo Scala, also dedicated himself to an alternative version of the same events, imitating two Greek models in particular, Plutarch's second-century *Parallel Lives* and Dionysius's *Roman Antiquities*, in order to give greater space to the most famous figures of archaic Florentine history (although they bordered on legend). Unfortunately, Scala's work was never finished and for a long time enjoyed limited manuscript circulation. Only the first six books survive today, in a 1677 edition.

Writing the official history of Florence was not among the chancellors' mandatory tasks, even though, after the reform of the city administration in 1483, the secretary was required to take notes of "the deeds of the Florentine people" in "annalistic form," that is, day by day. Nevertheless, given their required mastery of Latin, their access to the commune's archives, and their duty to protect the good reputation of the city through their official correspondence, it is not surprising that three of Machiavelli's predecessors undertook such an engaging commitment and that Machiavelli too was tempted by the same project. As a matter of fact, some of his handwritten fragments suggest that he, too, envisioned a similar work during his years in the chancery; the discovery in 2020 of one hundred unpublished pages he sketched in the years 1498 through 1515 partly with the help of his colleagues in the chancery reinforces the hypothesis that for some time Machiavelli thought of writing a summary of the most recent Florentine history.

Machiavelli came to historiography relatively late, however, and only thanks to the urging of his protectors from the Rucellai Gardens, who tried to get him a well-paid job and—even more importantly—to help him open a channel of communication with the Medici that *The Prince* had failed to establish years earlier. In the summer of 1520, Machiavelli therefore composed "as an experiment" a short biography of the fourteenth-century condottiere Castruccio Castracani of Lucca (dedicated to Zanobi Buondelmonti and Luigi Alamanni); a few months later, in November of the same year, the University of Pisa commissioned him to write a history of Florence (at his leisure, either in Latin or Italian); finally, Machiavelli offered the completed work to the new Medici pontiff Clement VII, in 1525.

Since he obviously could not avoid commenting on the Medici, Machiavelli had to weigh his words with extreme care. He confessed in a letter to his friend Guicciardini: "I would pay ten pennies, I do not want to say more, to have you here so that I could show you where I am, because, having to come to certain particulars, I would need to understand from you if I offend either by exalting or by lowering too much; but I will keep myself advised, and I will do things in such a way that, in my telling the truth, no one will be aggrieved" (August 30, 1524). A shrewd reader, however, would have been able to read between the lines of his judgment, as Machiavelli revealed to a dear friend from the Rucellai Gardens, the younger political theorist Donato Giannotti:

> Regarding his sincerity, he [Machiavelli] told me these exact words: "I cannot write these *Histories* from Cosimo's seizure of power to Lorenzo's death as I would if I were free of any caution: the actions will be true and I will not omit anything, I will only avoid the discussion of the causes of the things; for example, I will tell the events and the things that happened when Cosimo took the state, but I won't say in which way and with which means and cunning one reaches such a height, and, for whoever wants to understand that, note very well what I will make his adversaries say, because what I do not want to say explicitly, I will make his adversaries say."
>
> (Donato Giannotti to Marcantonio Michiel, June 30, 1533)

This is a confirmation, among other things, of the special importance that speeches hold in Machiavelli's historiography (apparently the stratagem worked well: Clement VII appreciated the *Florentine Histories* very much).

Although written in Italian, the *Florentine Histories* belong in every respect to humanistic historiography. They not only follow all the formal conventions of the genre (notably, the yearly organization of the narrative, the fictitious speeches, the most important figures' portraits at the time of their death, the careful selection of the subject matter . . .), but they also explicitly engage in dialogue with Bruni's work (first of all in its ambition to cover the entire history of Florence, which in the case of Machiavelli goes up to 1492, the year of Lorenzo the Magnificent's death). At the same time, however, the *Florentine Histories* apply the standard apparatus of humanist historiography to an idiosyncratic reading of the city's past and do not refrain from a harsh polemic against Bruni and Bracciolini. In the opening pages both predecessors are accused of having neglected the role that internal divisions played in Florence and of having therefore overlooked one of the main reasons for its failure in what was a softened and euphemistic representation of its past. Indeed, according to Machiavelli, their silence on such a crucial topic persuaded him to begin his narrative at a much earlier chronological point instead of starting with the Medici's ascendency in 1434 (as he had originally planned), in order to fill this gap and amend their inaccurate judgments.

Likewise, undertaking the new task, Machiavelli did not lose his interest in political theory. Quite the contrary: the *Florentine Histories* should be read as the last important segment of his reflection on politics—as they have often been read by later thinkers (like Karl Marx, Alexis de Tocqueville, and Simone Weil). Even more important, thanks to the *Florentine Histories'* broad international circulation, the vicissitudes of Machiavelli's homeland have become almost as present in the Western political imagination as those of Rome, Sparta, and Athens.

The theoretical drive of Machiavelli's work can be easily perceived through a quick comparison with vernacular chronicles and humanist histories. In order to avoid reducing the narrative to a plain sequence of events, each book opens with a sort of *overture* that draws the readers' attention to what, in Machiavelli's view, will be the main topic of the following pages. This procedure is unparalleled among classical and fourteenth- and fifteenth-century authors, and it is clearly designed to highlight the relevant political lessons to be drawn from the narrative. Proceeding in order through the eight books, readers encounter praise of the usefulness of the Roman colonies (2.1); a comparison between Rome's innocuous tumults and Florence's bloody feuds and riots (3.1, where Machiavelli also commends Roman learning-by-doing, implicitly endorsing it as an alternative to humanist political pedagogy); an analysis of the need for cities that lacked a solid constitution to rely on prudent citizens who offset that original defect (4.1); an examination of the causal relationship between virtue and quiet, quiet and idleness, idleness and disorder, disorder and ruin, ruin and order, and—in a circular fashion—order and virtue (the last one being the mother of "glory" and "good fortune") (5.1); a lamentation of the mercenary armies' flaws (6.1); a comparative assessment of (good) divisions "without sects" and (bad) divisions "with sects" (7.1); and an appraisal of the failed conspiracies' deleterious effects (8.1).

The *Florentine Histories* can be divided approximately into three parts. Like a preamble, book 1 summarizes Italian history from the fall of the Roman Empire to the beginning of the fifteenth century, focusing mainly on the popes' errors and their responsibility for the present political weaknesses of the peninsula (interestingly enough, its Latin translation would have wide autonomous circulation in Lutheran Europe). Books 2–4 then recount Florentine events from 1215 to 1434. In particular, starting from the feud between the Donati and Buondelmonti families that, according to civic chronicles, inflamed Florence's

internal discord, book 2 tells of the divisions between different
factions (feudal magnates and people, Guelphs and Ghibellines,
White Guelphs and Black Guelphs), and it culminates in the
story of the so-called duke of Athens, a French aristocrat who
managed to make himself lord of the commune for less than a
year (1342–1343) but was then quickly expelled after the entire
city rose in arms against him. Following the same line of thought,
book 3 dwells on the conflicts inside the Florentine elite that in
1378 provoked the insurrection of the poorest wool workers, the
so-called Ciompi. The final defeat of the Ciompi in 1383 paved
the way for an increasingly oligarchic government that lasted for
some decades, while book 4 centers on the Medici's progressive
seizure of power and the fortunate circumstances that led Cosimo's faction to prevail over its opponents. The third part of the
work (books 5–8) concentrates instead on more recent events,
which are largely left out of Bruni's, Bracciolini's, and Scala's
histories. Here much room is given to criticism of the Medici
regime, for example through a heartfelt speech by their adver-
sary Rinaldo degli Albizzi, who from exile tried to persuade the
duke of Milan, Francesco Sforza, to take up arms in order to
free Florence of Cosimo's tyranny (*Florentine Histories* 5.8). This
is probably one of the passages Machiavelli was referring to in
Giannotti's letter quoted earlier.

All the characteristic features of Machiavelli's historiography—
his special attention to internal conflicts, his "critical" use of
direct speeches, his recourse to Rome as an (explicit or implicit)
yardstick of comparison—converge in one of the most famous
passages of the work: the long oration given by a Ciompo on
the eve of the second insurrection of 1378, when the most radical wing of the movement was defeated by an alliance of the

rest of the people and the oligarchy after a violent clash in the street. Largely inspired by a short Latin tract by a Neapolitan humanist (the epistle *De nobilitate* of Antonio de' Ferraris, better known as Galateo, where a man of obscure origin derides the moral scruples of the masses and exposes the merciless violence on which the power of the self-proclaimed nobility relies), even today the radicalism of the Ciompo's eloquent speech continues to impress readers. The "plebeian" (as Machiavelli calls the anonymous speaker) argues that the only way to be forgiven for past violence is to double it; that clothing alone distinguishes the nobles from the non-nobles ("undress us naked, you will see us similar; cover us with their clothes and them with ours: undoubtedly we will seem noble, and they ignoble"); that all the wealth accumulated by prosperous citizens is the fruit of their own or their ancestors' robberies, because the "good" and the "faithful" are always destined to succumb to the "rapacious" and the "fraudulent," who, once enriched, "under the false name of gain, will make" their thefts "look honest"; and that, for all these reasons, the Ciompi should not hesitate to strike at their enemies because "those who win, in whatever way they win, never bring back shame" and "where there is fear of hunger and of prison, as there is in us, fear of Hell cannot nor should have a place" (*Florentine Histories* 3.13).

It is a remarkable piece of prose, but an unsettling one, that tests the interpretive skills of his readers. At the end of the speech, Machiavelli immediately makes it clear that he does not approve of the Ciompo's address by writing that he "greatly inflamed minds already disposed to mischief" (while, just a few pages before, in *Florentine Histories* 3.11, he had praised the Standardbearer Luigi Guicciardini's efforts to win a compromise with the agitators). As the provocative attitude of the proletarian leader here and there echoes the disillusioned approach to politics of *The Prince* and the *Discourses*, many scholars have thought that behind him we should recognize the author's ideas and feelings, but this interpretation is unlikely also in light of Machiavelli's constant criticism of Florence's un-Roman (that is, violent) internal struggles. Other scholars have favored a different reading: that, by making the Ciompo and the standard-bearer speak in sequence, Machiavelli merely wanted to express the ideas and sentiments behind each of the conflicting driving forces of history in fourteenth-century Florence without taking sides—so to speak from a higher, overarching perspective. This second interpretation is preferable, for it is closer to the overall design of book 3 and to the way Renaissance historiography works. This is, however, only part of the explanation. Machiavelli explicitly characterizes the Ciompi's self-destructing insurrection as a dead end, but he is especially interested in what the victims of extreme labor exploitation in Florence's preindustrial factories see, and he uses their uncompromising hostility toward the ruling class to demystify the oligarchic nature of the Florentine republican tradition. In doing this, Machiavelli imitates the Latin historians, who often gave voice to the subjugated peoples' allegations against their oppressors in order to denounce Roman imperialism (starting, notably, with Calgacus, the valiant commander of the Britons in Tacitus's short biography *Agricola* 30–32, but the same literary device can also be found in other ancient historians, from Sallust to Curtius Rufus). Like them, Machiavelli thinks that only the most hardcore enemies actually know the whole truth about those they plan to annihilate. Pressured by necessity, they have a more acute understanding of the situation, and it is their greater perceptiveness that makes their point of view so precious for somebody who tries to unveil how a political system actually works—even if that does not necessarily mean that they are right and that the historian approves of their deeds. Just as the victims of Roman dominion detected better than anybody else that an economy relying on a massive exploitation of slaves needs constant wars of conquest to recruit new labor, the Ciompo is ideally positioned to expose the invisible roots of Florence's magnificence and strength—that is, a relentless and violent abuse of the working class incomparable with the treatment of the plebeians by the patricians in Rome (on this subject, it must be remembered that Renaissance Florence was probably the richest city in Europe but also one of the most socially unequal). According to Machiavelli (who is always interested in the economic side of power relations), the proletarians of the Wool Guild are treated like enslaved foreigners, not like fellow citizens, and this is the reason why they are so unwilling to find any sort of agreement with their exploiters. In the long run, such internecine strife can only destroy Florence, but the responsibility for this fight without possible resolution must be assigned first and foremost to the aristocrats' greed. From this perspective, even if the Ciompo's solution is blatantly mistaken (because lethal for everybody), his awareness of the evils of Florence could not be fuller. Why? Because, for Machiavelli, truth is not the result of detached observation but of intellectual commitment nourished by conflict.

The *Florentine Histories* are a work of recapitulation, which from a strictly theoretical viewpoint adds little to Machiavelli's previous thinking. However, the continuous reference to topics already discussed in earlier texts should not be considered a weakness, since the difficulties of his own city provide him with a great number of examples confirming his theses—a bit like a scientist who, in order to verify a hypothesis, repeats an experiment with other sample data. From any point of view, republican Rome and Florence could not be further apart. Overall, then, the eight books addressed to Clement VII tell a story of failure despite the promising beginning. Contrary to his civic tradition, which exalted Florence's Roman origins, Machiavelli is unsparing in his criticism, as only Dante and the fifteenth-century chronicler Giovanni Cavalcanti (not coincidentally a source much used in the third part of the *Florentine Histories*) had done before him. Instead of being the most glorious daughter of Rome, and one destined by her birth for a great future, in Machiavelli's narrative Florence instead amounts to an ugly degenerate copy of her ancestor. And as Rome represents in the *Discourses* the model to be followed, with its selfless commanders, its invincible army, its plebs both combative and reasonable, its institutions perfectly conceived to resist any unexpected event, here Florence is summoned to impart only negative lessons.

As already seen, the humanists habitually taught that bad models were no less valuable than good ones because they helped readers recognize the road that should not be taken. Knowing how a tyrant acts, by contrast, teaches the opposite ways in which a true prince must behave, but the same principle applies in every field. As Machiavelli too once wrote to Guicciardini in apparent paradox: "I believe that this would be the true way to go to Paradise: to learn the way to Hell in order to escape it" (May 17, 1521). For Florence, evidently, something similar can be said. At least in Machiavelli's history his homeland constantly embodies the antimodel that, in a sort of reverse proof, confirms the necessity for the moderns to change course and take up the teaching of Rome. By reasserting and reinforcing the teachings of his previous works, Machiavelli's inquiry into Florence's failures is therefore the perfect culmination of his intellectual journey.

5

Beyond

> *No history could illustrate better than that of the reputation of Machiavelli the triviality and the irrelevance of influence. His message has been falsified by persistent romanticism ever since. To the humbug of every century Machiavelli is essential. And yet no great man has been so completely misunderstood. He is always placed a little askew. He does not belong with Aristotle, or with Dante, in political theory; he attempted something different. He does not belong with Napoleon, and still less with Nietzsche. His statements lend themselves to any modern theory of the State, but they belong with none.*
>
> —Thomas Sterling Eliot, *Niccolò Machiavelli*

A Contested Legacy (1523–1539)

No television series on the Italian Renaissance misses an opportunity to evoke his innumerable perfidies. An adjective derived from his surname summarizes all the vices assigned to politicians ("Machiavellian"). In English, his first name is associated with none other than the devil ("Old Nick"). A late twentieth-century American gangsta rapper, Tupac Shakur, after reading *The Prince* in prison, referred to him for one of his various pseudonyms ("Makaveli") . . . No doubt about it: even today, among the general public, Machiavelli still struggles with the black legend that has accompanied him for half a millennium.

"The problem with Machiavelli is that the name carries so much baggage," the Indian-born Anglo-American novelist Salman Rushdie once said in an interview about his *The Enchantress of Florence* (2008), where the chancellor of the republic is one of the leading characters (after making an appearance in historical novels like George Eliot's *Romola*, 1862–1863, and W. Somerset Maugham's *Then and Now*, 1946, and inspiring the title of H. G. Wells's contemporary political satire *The New Machiavelli*, 1911). Yet this is not the only obstacle to an unprejudiced reading of *The Prince* and the *Discourses*. The greatest arise as much from open counterfeits as from worn-out formulas. Faced with these less visible but more powerful distortions, it is important to recall that *no*, in fact, Machiavelli did not "separate politics from ethics," nor did he proclaim that "the ends justify the means" (just to take two banal examples). There was a precise moment when these and other successful slogans began to circulate, and understanding how and why that happened (that is, amid what political and cultural battles) remains the best way to avoid such misleading formulations. Aside from their historical relevance (who could deny that these apocryphal Machiavellis have left a footprint no less profound than the true Machiavelli?), the study of these clichés is thereby unavoidable for those who aspire to read his writings without preconceptions.

Probably one of the most significant aspects of Machiavelli's afterlife is the great number of opposing interpretations to which he was subjected just after his death or even while he was still alive: a sign of immediate interest but also the proof of an evident difficulty in understanding his work. Between 1523 and 1539, from Naples to Rome and from France to England, no fewer than five alternative readings can be discerned, all of them destined to influence subsequent debate. This timeline is even more meaningful if we consider the year of publication of Machiavelli's major works (all posthumous apart from *The Art of War* and *The Mandrake*). In 1531, the *Discourses* were in fact printed for the first time by Antonio Blado in Rome and by Bernardo Giunti in Florence, while a year later the same typographers brought out *The Prince* and the *Florentine Histories* (along with some minor pamphlets). Thanks to the circulation of manuscript copies, however, the battle over Machiavelli's intellectual legacy had at that point already been underway for some years. A careful examination of these early readings is therefore essential to pondering any ensuing interpretations.

Machiavelli the Antiaristocratic Theorist of Absolutism

The first evidence of *The Prince*'s dissemination outside Tuscany is linked to the name of Agostino Nifo, a renowned Aristotelian philosopher from the Kingdom of Naples. In 1522, after teaching for some years in Padua, Naples, Rome, and Pisa (where he was seemingly the best-paid professor of philosophy on the whole continent), Nifo returned to his native province and, at the beginning of 1523, published a brief treatise for Emperor Charles V, the *De regnandi peritia*, which spawned one of the greatest misunderstandings in Machiavelli studies. Despite the fact that Nifo condemns almost all of the conclusions reached in *The Prince*, since the nineteenth century the *De regnandi peritia* has been wrongly characterized as plagiarism of the work against which it was composed because of the very large number of extensive literal quotations from Machiavelli's text. In reality, the tract is anything but that. In previous years, Nifo had become famous thanks to a series of philosophical diatribes (among which was a harsh attack undertaken at the explicit request of Leo X against Pietro Pomponazzi's freethinking *De immortalitate animae*), and the *De regnandi peritia* follows the same method of discussion. As in a university debate of the time, here Nifo presents *The Prince*'s propositions one by one (which explains his generous citations) before refuting the concessions that Machiavelli had made in the name of necessity and reaffirming Aristotle's traditional view about the actions that differentiate a good prince from a wicked tyrant. But why such interest in an author then unknown in Naples and who is only mentioned through a series of periphrases in the *De regnandi peritia*? The answer can only be that, in Machiavelli's "mirror," Nifo must have seen something particularly alarming even for those who lived outside Florence. In fact, a series of references scattered throughout the *De regnandi peritia* makes clear that Nifo interprets *The Prince* in the light of Neapolitan politics, with its decades-long conflict between the king and the great nobility to which Nifo's powerful protector, Ferrante Sanseverino, prince of Salerno, belonged. Shoehorned into a monarchical context that was foreign to the one in which it had been conceived, Machiavelli's treatise could easily sound like an attack on the feudal aristocracy. After all, did it not proclaim the ruler's rights to perform any action, even in defiance of religion and customary law, under the pretext of his precarious condition as a "new prince" (which, to some extent, Charles V could still consider himself to be in Naples)? From this perspective, *The Prince* would have amounted to a particularly extreme theorization of royal absolutism; hence Nifo must have felt called upon to refute its theses because no other political thinker had ever gone so far as presenting the monarch as omnipotent. In other words, even if Machiavelli was scarcely known outside Florence at that time, *The Prince* was an ideal target because—in light of Nifo's preoccupations—its scandalous conclusions about the legitimacy of violence, the dangers of "liberality," the importance of fear, and the right to simulate and deceive could be interpreted as the inevitable outcome of any unrestrained princely power. By denouncing Machiavelli in a tract addressed to Charles V, Nifo intended to warn the emperor of the risks to which he would have exposed himself had he followed the advice of his counselors in Madrid and Naples, who suggested he should further centralize Neapolitan government (and this is also the reason why the killing of Julius Caesar is so often mentioned in the text with approval—as a kind of indirect menace). Of course, this was not the real message of *The Prince*, which attacked a kind of informal aristocracy of money very different from the feudal lordships of the Kingdom of Naples. Nevertheless, it is noteworthy that, independently of Nifo (whose *De regnandi peritia* circulated little), in the following centuries Machiavelli would often be misunderstood in similar ways by readers accustomed to a monarchical system and therefore ready to mistake him for an especially intransigent theorist of the sovereign's *absoluta potestas* (absolute power)—if not simply a friend of tyrants (in the case of those who opposed the concentration of all the authority in the hands of the king).

Machiavelli the Plebeian Constitutionalist

In 1521 Machiavelli befriended a younger Florentine aristocrat: the jurist Francesco Guicciardini, who was born in 1483 and grew into the greatest sixteenth-century European historian with his twenty-book *History of Italy* (focused on the wars that had devastated the peninsula from 1494 to 1534 and published posthumously only in 1561–1564). In 1512, when he was ambassador to Spain on behalf of the Florentine republic, Guicciardini had composed a brief treatise on its institutions known as the *Discourse of Logroño* (from the town where it was written), which testifies to his considerable gifts as a political theorist and his ability to translate his elitist convictions into an organic project for his republic's reform. But when his friendship with Machiavelli gave him access to the still unpublished manuscripts of *The Prince* and the *Discourses*, the complexity and richness of Guicciardini's reflections significantly increased, as can easily be seen from the *Dialogue on the Government of Florence* (composed between 1521 and 1525), where Machiavelli's commentary on Livy offered him a lens through which to observe his city's recent vicissitudes and to imagine a strategy for recovery had the Medici lost their grip on the republic. From this moment on, Machiavelli's writings represented for the mature Guicciardini an intellectual challenge of the first order, to which he had to respond first of all by clarifying his own ideas (none of his theoretical works was published during his lifetime, and only in the mid-nineteenth century did his treatises find their way into print). Machiavelli's enormous influence is apparent on each page; at the same time, however, Guicciardini struggled to shield his preference for "narrow government" from the *Discourses'* devastating criticism of aristocratic Sparta and Venice. It was not just an abstract question, especially since between 1527 and 1530, when the republic of the Great Council was revived in Florence (before Charles V crushed it and reinstated the Medici), radical leaders like Pierfilippo Pandolfini widely drew on Machiavelli's lesson about the militia in a clearly antioligarchic fashion. The most important testimony of Guicciardini's intellectual skirmish with his friend is therefore found in the *Considerations on Machiavelli's Discourses*, which were composed in 1530. Here Guicciardini proceeds systematically, chapter by chapter, noting every objection and, whenever possible, providing an alternative reading of the same passages of Livy with his sound expertise in Roman law. Often the result of this effort is to think simultaneously both *with* and *against* Machiavelli, as if in a photographic negative of the original. For example, the *Considerations* praise Venice's and Sparta's concord while condemning Rome's plebeian unrest, popular trials, and the generous granting of citizenship to aliens. In short, Guicciardini tries to contain the *Discourses'* disruptive novelty by "purifying" Machiavelli's republican theory of its pro-popular elements in order to reconcile it with Cicero's and Aristotle's. As the saying goes: old wine in new barrels. But the importance of such an ambitious and close examination also lies in its foresight: independently of Guicciardini (whose political treatises had no circulation before 1857), it is in fact in this moderate key that Machiavelli's constitutional engineering would often be reworked in subsequent centuries (as in James Harrington, Montesquieu, and the American Founding Fathers).

Machiavelli the Cold Political Scientist

In the first Florentine edition of *The Prince*, which was dedicated to the powerful priest Giovanni Gaddi (who promoted its printing), the publisher Giunti invited Gaddi to defend the book "from those who are tearing it apart every day because of its subject, not knowing that those who teach herbs and medicines, also teach poisons, just so that, knowing them, we can protect ourselves from them; nor do they realize that there is no art nor science that cannot be used badly by those who are bad." These few lines are significant because they confirm that Machiavelli's detractors had already begun to make their voices heard in Florence. No less significant, however, is the typographer's justification. To validate Machiavelli's praise for fraud, deceit, and violence as acceptable instruments of rule, Giunti applies to *The Prince* an argument already employed by Aristotle in his vindication of rhetoric, according to which accomplished orators must handle all the tricks of the art of speech making just like good physicians must know harmful substances and antidotes in order to heal their patients (*Rhetoric* 1.1; see also Quintilian, *De institutione oratoria* 2.16); the same would be true for Machiavelli's teachings, in the sense that they are devoid of any moral or immoral connotation because they are merely "scientific." *The Prince* would therefore only offer a cold, ethically neutral examination of the instruments that work best for the seizure of power, communicating them to good princes as well as to their corrupt equivalents (again like Aristotle, who in *Politics* 5.11 presents the "remedies" through which even tyrants can preserve their wicked government without implying approval of their behavior). As the German philosopher Arthur Schopenhauer wrote much later, proposing another comparison that would be very successful: "To reproach Machiavelli for his work's immorality is as appropriate as it would be to reproach a fencing master for not beginning his lesson with a moral lecture against murder and killing" (*The World as Will and Representation*, 1819). In light of such an interpretation, notwithstanding the final exhortation to free Italy, Machiavelli's "mirror" would be nothing more than a dispassionate scrutiny of a particular type of ruler previously neglected by theory: the "new prince."

Machiavelli the Antichrist

Around 1539, probably while he was residing in southern France, the English cardinal Reginald Pole composed a violent attack on the king of England, Henry VIII: the *Apologia ad Carolum V*, which was addressed to the emperor but remained unpublished until 1744. Among the many crimes of which Pole accused his sovereign was the charge that he had embraced the Protestant Reformation only to free himself from the church's spiritual guidance and to rule in defiance of any moral principle; in doing so, Pole wrote, Henry had done nothing but follow the suggestions of his secretary and minister Thomas Cromwell, who in turn had been inspired by *The Prince*'s perverse doctrine. In the most rhetorically elaborate passage of the work, the long speech that Cromwell supposedly delivered to Pole to explain what he had learned from Machiavelli, we read: "'If the concept of honesty changes according to the opinion of men, is it more lawful that this happens by their will than by the will of princes, whose deliberations must be held by law? By the decision of princes even laws which are reputed to be immutable have been dissolved.'" Here begins the legend of the diabolical Machiavelli: for Pole, in fact, both *The Prince* and Henry are unmistakable signs of the coming of the Antichrist (perhaps the king of England himself). At the same time, however, apart from the characterization of Machiavelli as a satanic thinker (which is peculiar to Pole), the proximity of the *Apologia* to Nifo's *De regnandi peritia* is striking. In both treatises, the danger of *The Prince* resides in the elimination of all the limits that had traditionally been imposed on the sovereigns' arbitrary will, and tellingly their attacks end up converging (although Nifo derives the ruler's immorality from the absence of any political restriction while Pole proceeds in the opposite direction by recognizing the embryo of "tyranny" in the dismissal of religious authority). It is also significant, from this point of view, that both warnings were dispatched to the same addressee: no less than Emperor Charles V, who, at that time, still embodied the highest political authority in the Christian world.

Machiavelli the Faithful Republican in Disguise

Pole's *Apologia* also bears traces of a further reading that was widespread after the publication of *The Prince* and the *Discourses*. This is precious testimony because it shows how the Florentines had already at that point begun to wonder about the apparent discrepancies between these two works. The *Apologia* tells us that when, in 1537, Pole had traveled to Florence (where he met with Guicciardini, among others), here some of Machiavelli's friends and advocates explained to him that the former secretary had remained a convinced republican all his life and that even *The Prince* should be read in this light. Machiavelli, Pole's informants argued, could not be unaware that both Aristotle (*Politics* 5.8) and Seneca (*De clementia* 1.11.4) taught that no form of government lasts a shorter time than tyranny: hence, the Florentine's obvious conclusion was that, with his despicable lessons of despotism, Machiavelli had just tried to lead Lorenzo astray in order to speed up the Medici's fall and the restoration of popular government. According to such "oblique interpretation" (as it would be called later), *The Prince* ought thus to be read against the grain: it would be a Trojan horse. Relaunched some decades later by the great theorist of international relations and regius professor of civil law at Oxford, Alberico Gentili (*De legationibus* 3.8–9, 1585), this reading would become mainstream in the eighteenth century. Yet, in authors such as Baruch Spinoza (*Tractatus politicus* 5.7, published posthumously in 1677), Jean-Jacques Rousseau (*The Social Contract* 3.6, 1762), and Vittorio Alfieri (*The Prince and Letters* 2.9, 1786), the thesis would take a slightly different form: for them, Machiavelli sought not to deceive Lorenzo but to make all his readers realize that a bloodthirsty despot always lurks even behind the best prince, because it is autocracy in all its facets that is corrupt at its very core and that has the power to pervert even the finest souls. It is worth noting, however, that in this case too the first seeds of one of the readings destined to mark Machiavelli's interpretation in subsequent centuries already circulated a few years after his death.

Condemnations and Adaptations (1540–1815)

As Pole's work demonstrates, Machiavelli's fame very soon crossed the Alps. Just as had happened to Rome after the subjugation of Greece (Horace, *Epistles* 2.1, vv. 156–57: "Conquered Greece took captive her savage conqueror and / brought her arts into rustic Latium"), the powerful Spanish and French monarchies, which fought in the Italian peninsula for more than half a century in order to impose their supremacy over the entire continent (1494–1559), rapidly adopted Italy's new classicizing culture. Within the "Italian wave" that from France and Spain disseminated the achievements of the Renaissance all over Europe, Machiavelli was one of the authors who enjoyed the greatest and most lasting success, along with Petrarch, Boccaccio, Sannazaro (with his pastoral prosimetrum *Arcadia*, 1504), Ariosto, Guicciardini, and Baldassarre Castiglione (with his *Book of the Courtier*, 1528). A small chart showing the year of the first printed translation of Machiavelli's writings in the main European languages helps us follow the diffusion of his ideas in different geographical areas (table 5.1).

Even if this data must be handled with due caution, some clear tendencies emerge. It is impossible not to notice, for example, the immediate interest in *The Art of War* and, on the other hand, the belated translation of *The Mandrake* (even if the text was well known outside Italy, as proved by the French poet Jean de la Fontaine's verse rewriting in his *Contes*, 1671). Geographically, the

Table 5.1. First printed translations

	Latin	Castilian	English	French	German	
The Mandrake (c. 1520)	no	1916	1927	**1729**	1805	1729–1927
The Art of War (1521)	1610	**1536***	1560	1546	1619	**1536–1619**
The Discourses on Livy (1531)	1588	1552	1636	1544** **1548**	1776	1544–1776
The Prince (1532)	1560	1821	1640	**1553**	1714	1553–1821
The Florentine Histories (1532)	1564*** 1610	1892	1595	**1577**	1788	1564–1892
(*The Mandrake* excluded)	1560–1610	1536–1892	1560–1640	**1544–1577**	1619–1788	

Note: First complete translation of each work is noted by bold text.

*A plagiarism by Diego de Salazar.

**Only book 1. A French translation of the whole work was published only in 1548.

***Only book 1. A Latin translation of the whole work was published only in 1610.

centrality of France stands out. Spain, on the contrary, quickly loses its initial supremacy as a consequence of the Council of Trent (1545–1563), and Germany arrives very late (conversely, both *The Prince* and the *Discourses* were already translated into Dutch in 1615). Some other considerations, however, complicate this first picture: the wide diffusion of the Italian language, at that time the lingua franca of culture in Europe; the enduring importance of Latin as the idiom of communication among scholars and scientists, especially in central, northern, and eastern Europe (hence the delay of the German versions); and the circulation of manu-script translations decades or even centuries in advance of the first printing (a phenomenon particularly significant in England and Spain, where, for instance, in 1680 the Spanish king Charles II commissioned a Castilian version of *The Prince* for his own pri-vate use so that he could more easily read the treatise, which at that time was still suppressed in Catholic countries). In short, printed editions alone only partially account for the manifold propagation of Machiavelli's ideas across the continent.

In this multifarious tradition, at least seven fundamental trends are clearly recognizable from the mid-sixteenth century to the end of the eighteenth century, as follows.

The Atheist Friend of Tyrants

We are well informed about Machiavelli's irreligiosity by his contemporaries. In addition to his works, all the most reliable sources concur (often playfully deriding him for his bad reputa-tion), from the Florentine aristocrat Alamanno Salviati (who in a 1507 letter wrote to Machiavelli: "I do not think that you com-pletely lack faith, but I am certain that you do not have much left") to Francesco Vettori (who in a 1513 epistle remarked: "On festive days I go to the Mass, and I do not do like you, who sometimes neglect it"), and from Francesco Guicciardini (who, in a 1521 letter, laughed at the fact that the republic had sent a well-known unbeliever like Machiavelli to select a preacher, say-ing that it was like asking a notorious homosexual to choose the appropriate bride for somebody else and who, in a 1527 mis-sive, ironically suggested that Machiavelli should not change the habitual course of his life and start caring for his soul, "for, having always professed a different creed," at that point a conversion "would be attributed rather to dementia than to goodness") to his brother Luigi (who in his dialogue *On Man's Free Will*, composed around 1533, presents Machiavelli as a denier of divine providence) and the physician, historian, and bishop of Nocera Paolo Giovio (who had met Machiavelli in the Rucellai Gardens in the 1520s and later described him as "a mocker and an atheist" in his *Elogia*, 1546). It is not surprising, therefore, that Machiavelli's work was one of the first victims of the Catholic response to the Protestant Reformation. The 1531–1532 Roman edition appeared with a printing privilege from Pope Clement VII, but in 1559 Machiavelli was included in the strictest category of the first *Index of Forbidden Books* (where he would remain until its suppression, in 1966), with a prohibition not just on reading his writings but even on mentioning his name. Thus, until the eighteenth century, when the Enlightenment made the *Index* less effective, most of Machiavelli's editions (even in the original language) were produced outside Italy, where controls were laxer and therefore where a rich market of clandestine books flourished, often with false bibliographical data (the name of the publisher and the place and date of impression).

However, hostility toward Machiavelli was not confined to Catholic Europe. Among Protestants, the French Huguenot jurist Innocent Gentillet enjoyed extraordinary success with his *Anti-Machiavel* (1578), in which he accused Machiavelli of having inspired Charles IX of France to instigate the massacre of Saint Bartholomew (when, on the night of August 24, 1572, thousands of unarmed French Calvinists were murdered at their sovereign's behest because of their faith). The fact that the king's mother, Catherine de' Medici, was Florentine represented for Gentillet proof that the tyrannical lessons of *The Prince* and the *Discourses* were now spreading everywhere from Italy. Although Gentillet's reading was very superficial, even caricatured, it is undeniable that in a first phase Machiavelli's thought penetrated northern Europe especially through his summary (his *Anti-Machiavel* was printed no fewer than nineteen times by 1655, with versions in Latin, English, and German). For instance, in the Elizabethan theater—from Christopher Marlowe (*The Jew of Malta*, 1590) to William Shakespeare (*Henry VI*, 1592; *The Merry Wives of Windsor*, 1602)—the character of Machiavelli displays all the diabolical traits of the teacher of evil. Particularly famous among the many attacks on *The Prince* is also another *Anti-Machiavel*, this one composed in French by the young king of Prussia Frederick II with the help of Voltaire (1740), whose no fewer than fifty editions appeared by 1796, in this case together with Machiavelli's text (also in German, English, Italian, and Dutch).

The Naturalist

The same religious skepticism that led to the church's prohibition of his works also fueled interest in Machiavelli. In *The Prince* and the *Discourses*, readers could find an entirely naturalized vision of man, one where elementary passions such as fear and desire dominate, where there is no place for the immortality of the soul, and where religion is reduced to a mere political tool (an *instrumentum regni*, instrument of government). In his

nonconformism Machiavelli became a model of the antidog-
matic use of reason, for example for the seventeenth-century
French scholars Gabriel Naudé and Pierre Bayle. Yet through
his naturalistic anthropology, Machiavelli influenced not just
authors who were politically close to him (such as Spinoza) but
also those who openly opposed his republican ideals and severely
condemned his admiration for ancient political models (such as
Hobbes). Along these lines, among the ideas of *The Prince* and
the *Discourses* that yielded lasting fruits we should remember the
suggestion that it is easier to build an ordered society on selfish
interests (because they are rational and therefore calculable) than
on passions, however noble (because they are unpredictable)—an
innovation whose legacy to seventeenth- and eighteenth-century
philosophy was later greatly valorized by the German-American
economist Albert O. Hirschman in *The Passions and the Interests: Political Arguments for Capitalism Before Its Triumph* (1977).

The Teacher of Method

Very soon, philosophers and political thinkers began to point to
Machiavelli as a master of method. Francis Bacon, for example,
noted several times that the *Discourses* had marked a turning
point, whereby an empirical-inductive approach to social facts
had replaced the medieval scholastic's predominantly deductive
one. Thus, in the wake of Bacon's *Advancement of Learning*
(1605), a long tradition (particularly strong between the early
nineteenth and mid-twentieth centuries) presented Machiavelli
as one of the fathers of modern science: "the Galileo of politics"

(a formula still repeated by Ernst Cassirer in *The Myth of the State*, published posthumously in 1946).

Yet, quite apart from Bacon's assertions, Machiavelli's methodological importance in Western thought is above all inseparable from the extraordinary success of the "discourse form," which, beginning in the 1560s, was taken up by some of the greatest seventeenth-century political thinkers (including Scipione Ammirato, Francisco de Quevedo, Virgilio Malvezzi, Algernon Sidney, Traiano Boccalini, and Nicolas Amelot de la Houssaye). Some glossed ancient authors (especially Caesar, Tacitus, and Plutarch, at a time when the European courts' interest had shifted from republican to imperial Rome), others focused their attention on modern ones (like Guicciardini, Bodin, and Giovanni Botero), but all of them followed in the footsteps of Machiavelli's commentary on Livy. Interestingly enough, the philosophical genre of the discourse was still practiced during the eighteenth century. For example, as late as 1790 the vice president of the United States, John Adams, composed his *Discourses on Davila*, a long treatise where Enrico Caterino Davila's history of the wars fought by Holland for independence (1630) is analyzed exactly as Machiavelli had done with Livy (but with the purpose of warning his fellow citizens about the dangers of a democracy without limits).

Moreover, the *Discourses* stimulated the birth of another literary genre that was destined to enjoy great success. Here Bacon's opinion is again useful. According to the *Advancement of Learning* (8.2), Machiavelli used the "discourse form" in two different ways, moving either from a concrete example or from a general question. Bacon prefers the first approach (because it is more akin to his own inductive method), but it is rather the chapters that centered on a broad problem and resolved it through discussion of a multiplicity of sources that shaped the new and original form of argumentation that we got accustomed to calling the "essay" in the wake of Michel de Montaigne's and Bacon's own *Essays* (respectively printed in 1580 and 1597). Today, this affiliation risks passing unnoticed, but for the first readers the fact that this new genre could be traced back to Machiavelli must have been so evident that, when Montaigne was translated into Italian, his book was presented under the title of *Saggi o discorsi* (1633), in order to make the genealogy explicit and appeal to a public already familiar with the "discourse form."

The Theorist of the Reason of State

The formula *ratio status regni* (or *ratio status regis*) has been used since the late Middle Ages to refer to the set of conditions necessary for a kingdom's preservation. In the sixteenth century, the expression began to spread into Italian (for instance, Guicciardini uses it), until it was canonized by the Jesuit Giovanni Botero's *Reason of State* in 1589. Even though the phrasing "reason of State" never appears in *The Prince* or the *Discourses*, Botero's extensive recourse to these works soon induced people to consider Machiavelli the true founder of this school of thought. Nevertheless, because the reason-of-State thinkers drew on his teachings without mentioning him directly (given the church's censorship), and because they alluded to him by speaking rather of Tacitus (the first-century Latin historian who had cast the corruption of the Roman Empire in so dark a light), Botero's followers were often referred to also as Tacitists. Much of the effort of these Tacitists was aimed at making their princes' power steadier, at limiting the use of violence and deception in interstate struggles (while recognizing their inevitability), and at reconciling Machiavelli's most infamous maxims with religious imperatives. Botero, for example, dreamed of a mild reason of State moderated by the church's spiritual authority (and in his writings elaborated with great ingenuity especially upon *The Prince*'s and the *Discourses*' insights on the social and economic factors of success and decay of cities), while in his posthumous *De arcanis rerum publicarum* (1605) the Lutheran German jurist Arnold Clapmar—in order to prevent any confusion on this delicate matter—proposed distinguishing between *arcana imperii*, "secrets of power" (legitimate, as they are aimed at the preservation of the whole community) and *arcana dominationis*, "secrets of domination" (illegitimate, as they are aimed at the success of the prince alone).

The Neo-Aristotelian

Machiavelli was often reproached for not having properly discriminated between the prince and the tyrant and for having attributed to the former also the "remedies" that were attached only to the latter in Aristotle's *Politics*. It is a criticism already present in Nifo and Gentillet but one also repeated by Botero (*On the Duty of the Cardinal*, 1598), by René Descartes in a letter to Princess Elisabeth of Bohemia (September 1646), by the German political thinker Hermann Conring (*Introductio in Politicam Aristotelis*, 1656), and by the German historian of philosophy Jacob Brucker (*Historia critica philosophiae* 4.2, 1744), among many others. However, the same similarities were also employed for the opposite reason, that is, to shield Machiavelli from the accusation of promoting immoral behaviors among the rulers. In fact, according to the German Jesuit Kaspar Schoppe (*Paedia politices*, 1623), Naudé (*Political Considerations on Coups d'État*, 1639), and Bayle (*Historical and Critical Dictionary*, 1695–1696), Machiavelli was just a modern Aristotle, who, for the sake of scientific knowledge (and exhaustivity), did not refrain from describing the actions of both good and corrupt princes but who did not intend to legitimize the second. After all, if even a saint of the church like Thomas Aquinas had rewritten and endorsed the same passages from the *Politics*, how could Machiavelli be blamed for the identical action?

The Theorist of Mixed Government

One of Machiavelli's main legacies in European political thought is his way of discussing the Roman constitution as an organic whole. Behind Machiavelli, as we have seen, it is easy to recognize the pathbreaking lesson of Polybius and Dionysius; it was nonetheless the *Discourses* that stimulated the new approach, and their influence can easily be recognized in leading figures such as Donato Giannotti, Jean Bodin, Harrington, Sidney, Montesquieu, and Rousseau—all of whom often mention him and even more often silently draw inspiration from his works. Yet Machiavelli's legacy is also very strong in authors who do not directly refer to his writings, such as the antiquarian Carlo Sigonio in his *De republica Atheniensium* (1564), the first modern reconstruction of the Athenian political system, which was destined to shape the image of Greek democracy until the nineteenth century. Partly thanks to Montesquieu's mediation, the teachings of the *Discourses* would come to mark the discussion on checks and balances and the first wave of the modern constitutionalization process (the late eighteenth to mid-nineteenth century), with particular influence on the fundamental law of the United States (1787–1789). Probably the most significant feature of Machiavelli's copious afterlife as a theorist of forms of government and constitutional engineer, however, is that—as had already happened with Guicciardini—his lesson was almost always reworked in moderate terms, starting with the elimination of the magistracy that in the *Discourses* compensates for the excessive power of the wealthy, that is, the tribunes of the plebs (even if, on this point, a notable exception can be found in some South American constitutions).

The Revolutionary

Political thinkers attentive to balancing the different powers tend to be interested above all in the state's ordinary functioning. However, Machiavelli's lesson also accompanied all major Western revolutions: from Holland (1568–1648) to England (1642–1651) and from the United States (1775–1783) to France (1789–1799) and Italy (1796–1799). Even more than in *The Prince*, the insurgents found in the *Discourses* a legitimation of social conflicts and an eloquent defense of their right to rebel (before seeking, again in the *Discourses*, a guide to building the new republican political order). Quite exceptionally, Machiavelli was consequently—at the same time and without contradiction—a theorist of both institutional stability and (in the constituent phase, when a new political order struggles to impose itself), radical discontinuity. In particular, his appreciation for ancient Rome's popular tumults can be seen as a real turning point in the history of political thought that inspired some of the major seventeenth- and eighteenth-century theorists (Tommaso Campanella, Malvezzi, Sidney, Montesquieu, Gabriel Bonnot de Mably, Adam Ferguson, Rousseau, Alfieri, Adams, Thomas Jefferson . . .), before the founding role of conflict in politics was finally fully recognized during the nineteenth century both by liberals and Marxists.

—∞∞∞—

However, these are just the principal tendencies, for Machiavelli's influence is easily recognizable in the most diverse contexts and authors from the mid-sixteenth century to the end of the eighteenth century. Two minor (but very telling) examples will suffice to give an idea of the extension of his heritage. In 1668 a Polish student, Johann Henricus Neuman, published in Jena a thirty-page dissertation *Machiavellus sine Machiavello*, where he tried to prove that all the principles of government taught by Machiavelli predated him and were universal. To this end, he analyzed the recent Manchu conquest of China and the inauguration of the Qing dynasty (1644), showing that the different warlords, generals, and pretenders to the throne had in fact deployed exactly the same stratagems that are taught in *The Prince*—without having read it (an argument that Conring had already made before Neuman with Greek and Roman history and one that a few years later the German playwright and professor Christian Weise would apply to the illiterate farmers living in the countryside in his witty prose comedy *A Peasant Machiavelli*, 1681). Similarly, when, in 1602, the East India Company, the first joint-stock company in the world (directly sponsored by the Dutch government), started its lucrative trade with India, the business corporation's managers took inspiration from Machiavelli's description of how the Bank of San Giorgio (which collected Genoa's public debt) had ruled over the republic's colonies and exploited local resources in return for its loans (*Florentine Histories* 8.29). Hence, although in his writings Machiavelli never acknowledged the importance of the geographical discoveries of his time (in spite of the fact that one of his friends was the brother of Amerigo Vespucci, the Florentine sailor who gave his name to the American continent), both examples prove that very soon his ideas started traveling to the extreme edges of the world and were successfully employed to interpret—and mold—the new, unexpected realities that the Europeans had come to face in their military and commercial expansion.

In the Mirror of the French Revolution (1816–1945)

Many French revolutionaries were familiar with Machiavelli, in part because of the illuminist philosophers Montesquieu, Mably, and Rousseau, who had all drawn abundantly from him. In the first phase of the French Revolution, several ideas from *The Prince* and the *Discourses* were therefore taken up again and successfully reworked in France and Italy: for example, on the shortcomings of princely "liberality" (which impoverishes citizens while pretending to enrich them), on the importance of military conscription, on the necessity of civil religion, on the usefulness of popular trials, and on the positive effects of social conflicts. However, all these concepts were already widely present in the radical Enlightenment and were used in public discourse without any particular originality in the years after the storming of the Bastille (1789).

The real watershed in Machiavelli interpretations would come a few years later, at the moment of the reappraisal of the revolutionary experience following the Congress of Vienna (1815), in post-Napoleonic Europe. The French Revolution had precipitated a true upheaval, marking the end of Old Regime estate society (the nobility, the church, and the "Third Estate"), the rise of the bourgeoisie, and the imposition on the entire European continent of Napoleon's new Civil Code (1804), which sanctioned the abolition of feudalism and affirmed the equality of all citizens before the law. Yet the 1789 rift above all challenged the idea that monarchs held their title by God's sanction and, accordingly, enjoyed a special sacred legitimacy—a legitimacy that, on the other hand, bound them to respect the church's teachings. It was hardly by chance, therefore, that one of the first accusations leveled against the revolutionaries was that of "having separated politics from religion" (and from its ethical principles) by arrogating to themselves the right to legislate at will on whatever matter. As a result, when the Bourbons returned to the French throne (1815), reactionary propaganda began to insinuate that, in breaking with the centuries-old traditions of the kingdom, the revolutionaries had followed *The Prince*'s tyrannical propositions that gave rulers full freedom of action (the first use of the formula probably occurred in a pamphlet of

1816 by an obscure polemicist, F. de Mazères: *On Machiavelli and the Influence of His Doctrine Over the Opinions, the Mores, and French Politics During the Revolution*). Likewise, in the same period, a forgery by the reactionary Abbe Aimé Guillon of the fake handwritten comments that Napoleon supposedly had inscribed in his private copy of *The Prince* started circulating in print (1816).

These attacks had a curious effect, however. As sometimes happens in similar cases, the formula met with success, but it was soon claimed by those who supported the French Revolution and who wanted to see their ideas linked to such an illustrious ancestor—first in Germany with Friedrich Wolff's *Considerations on Machiavelli's Prince* (1828) and eventually also in France and Italy. From that moment on, then, the emancipation of politics from the tutelage of (Christian) morality was increasingly presented as one of the constitutive features of political modernity and traced back to Machiavelli with tones of approval.

Wolff and his followers were not alone. A few years earlier, in a series of texts beginning in 1798 that long remained unpublished, another supporter of the French Revolution, Georg Wilhelm Friedrich Hegel, had bolstered an even more extreme idea: the superior right of the state to perform *any* act—even in defiance of common morality and religion. As Hegel wrote in his *Jena Lectures* (1805) with an eye on contemporary events:

> Such a State is the simple absolute spirit, which is certain of itself and for which nothing is worth being determined that is not itself, no concept of good and evil, of shame and infamy, of treachery and deception. Machiavelli's *The Prince* is written

in this great sense, that, in the foundation of the State in general, what is called treacherous murder, perfidious deception, cruelty, etc., has no meaning of evil, but is reconciled with itself. . . . His country was trampled by the foreigner, devastated and deprived of independence; each nobleman, leader, city asserted its own sovereignty. The only way to establish the State was to eradicate these sovereignties.

For his merciless fight against Italy's little feudal powers, even Machiavelli's Cesare Borgia deserved praise as the prophet of the modern state. Thus, a few years later the same concept reappeared with greater abundance of historical details in Hegel's influential *Lectures on the Philosophy of History* (published posthumously in 1837):

A papal territory was formed. Here, too, an innumerable number of independent dynastic princes had risen; little by little they were all submitted to the sole rule of the pope. There certainly exists a moral right to submission, as we see from Machiavelli's famous writing, *The Prince*. This book has often been rejected with horror, because it is filled with the maxims of the cruelest tyranny; however, once *The Prince* is understood in the noble sense of the necessary foundation of the State, it is clear that Machiavelli set forth the principles on which it was inevitable to form the States in those particular circumstances. It was necessary to crush independent lords and lordships. Therefore, even if we cannot approve the means taught by Machiavelli as the only suitable and fully justified ones (since the most unscrupulous violence, all species of deception, assassination, etc., belong to them), nonetheless we are ready to admit that those dynastic princes could only be fought in that way in order to be overthrown.

In the name of future order and justice, almost everything became therefore acceptable. As we have seen, Roman law had already affirmed that in the face of an extraordinary threat it was legitimate to resort to exceptional means to protect the community from extinction, but by comparison Hegel's position sounds much more radical. Sixteenth-century Italy, in fact, is called upon to highlight what was in his eyes one of the essential characteristics of the new modern state that the French Revolution had revealed, but which—at least according to him—had already been foreseen by Machiavelli: the superiority of politics over ethics as a *normal* attribute of any truly sovereign state. Somehow, it was like turning Nifo's negative interpretation of *The Prince* as an absolutist tract into a positive one (even if, in Hegel's time, the *De regnandi peritia* was completely forgotten).

Clearly, Hegel was not thinking in the abstract: his concerns were first of all about Germany, which was still divided into dozens of tiny political entities and therefore particularly vulnerable. Nor was he the only one. In 1807 another leading exponent of German idealism, Johan Gottlieb Fichte, at a time when his country was occupied by Napoleon, also referred to *The Prince* to encourage his own compatriots to free their country from its oppressor (as in chapter 26). Generally speaking, after the French Revolution Machiavelli was seen more and more often as the thinker of innovations and radical discontinuities par excellence, even if the change *The Prince* advocated could vary significantly according to its interpreters. For instance, after the defeat of the Revolution of 1848 in continental Europe (the so-called Springtime of the Peoples against monarchic absolutism), the Italian émigré and republican philosopher Giuseppe Ferrari wrote a book in French on *Machiavelli, Judge of the Revolutions of Our Time* (1849), while, from his Swiss exile, the French republican scholar and journalist Edgar Quinet praised *The Prince* as "the *Marseillaise* anthem of the Renaissance" in a militant multivolume monograph on *The Italian Revolutions* (1852). Patriotic appeal to the unification of Italy remained, however, Machiavelli's most valued characteristic during the Risorgimento (1815–1870). And, when in 1870 Rome too was finally annexed to the young state (born only in 1861), the leading literary critic of the time, Francesco De Sanctis, who had paid for his liberal ideas with exile from the Kingdom of the Two Sicilies, inserted a reference to the definitive victory of the national cause in the chapter on Machiavelli that he was composing for his *History of Italian Literature* (1870–1871): "As I write, the bells are ringing out, announcing the entry of the Italians into Rome. The temporal power [of the pope] collapses. And people shout 'Hurrah!' for the unification of Italy. Glory be to Machiavelli."

If the nineteenth century witnessed Machiavelli's rehabilitation and triumph, in the 130 years between the Restoration (1815) and World War II (1939–1945) readers concentrated almost exclusively on *The Prince*, increasingly overlooking the *Discourses*. On the one hand, this happened probably also because of Machiavelli's continuous reference to the ancients, in a climate strongly marked by the Romantic polemic against classicism in the name of a radical downturn of aesthetic values that set the spontaneous force of creative genius over literary and artistic imitation (as George Byron used to say, for a poet "it is a bad thing to have too good a memory"). How could such a proudly modernizing culture appreciate a work that insisted so much on the need to follow in the footsteps of republican Rome? Apart from focusing on *The Prince* alone (where, in comparison with the *Discourses*, the ancient authors apparently are less central to the arguments of the tract), another potential solution was to highlight Machiavelli's break with the Christian and medieval past as much as possible, therefore dwelling on a different aspect of his classicizing ethos. This is precisely what Jacob Burckhardt did in his influential *Civilization of the Renaissance in Italy* (1860), where fifteenth- and sixteenth-century Italy was presented as a neopagan, "individualist" society, which opened the path to our modern sensibility. According to that great Swiss historian (who was also a friend and colleague of Friedrich Nietzsche at the University of Basel), it was then that, for the first time, rulers started to mold their states as freely as the sculptors plied their "works of art," without religious restrictions of any sort. Renaissance neopaganism made that shift possible, but Machiavelli played a major role in this epochal process, and Burckhardt greatly admired his dispassionate "objectivity" and "frankness," especially visible in *Discourses* 3.6, where conspiracies are analyzed from the opposite perspectives of the prince and the schemers ("He treats existing forces as living and active, takes a large and an accurate view of alternative possibilities, and seeks to mislead neither himself nor others"). Driven by the international acclaim for *The Civilization of the Renaissance in Italy*, probably no nineteenth-century reading of Machiavelli left such a profound mark in subsequent interpretations as Burckhardt's—except for Hegel's.

Yet Machiavelli's classicistic attitude toward the ancients was not the only impediment to a full appreciation of his work. The more political science and sociology won academic recognition and grew stronger, the more scholars started questioning his understanding of social phenomena. Thus, when the greatest Italian nineteenth-century political thinker, the theorist of the elites Gaetano Mosca, drew on the *Discourses* in his *Elements of Political Science* (1896–1923) for the idea that "in all republics, however arranged, there are never more than forty or fifty leading citizens" (*Discourses* 1.16), he simultaneously dismissed Machiavelli's approval of the mixed constitution, reproaching him for failing to understand that—under the most varied names—the essence of any government is always oligarchic (a fault that for Mosca was proof that Machiavelli had remained a prescientific thinker and an "artist" of politics in the negative sense of the expression). At least, the other great Italian theorist of elites Vilfredo Pareto (who later in his life became an ardent fascist) was more approving, and he even made allusion to chapter 18 of *The Prince* in his *The Mind and Society* (1916) in order to separate political actors into two groups: the innovators ("foxes"), who systematically resort to cunning (and who in economics correspond to speculators), and the traditionalists ("lions"), who rely instead on force (in the economic sphere similar to rentiers).

Generally speaking, in comparison with the vitality of debate in previous centuries, Machiavelli's image was enormously impoverished, although major political thinkers continued to read his writings with passion (Benjamin Constant, John Stuart Mill, Alexis de Tocqueville, Giuseppe Mazzini, Karl Marx,

Friedrich Nietzsche . . .). It was as if his work could be reduced to chapters 6–8, 15–18, and 26 of *The Prince*, with Machiavelli concerned solely with the relationship between ethics and politics and the need to unify Italy at any cost (two themes often played in an anti-Catholic key during these years, given the church's opposition to the Risorgimento). Despite the pompous celebrations of Machiavelli as the forerunner of national state building during his centenary in 1869 and despite the first erudite research on his life and thought (the biographies by Francesco Saverio Nitti, Pasquale Villari, and Oreste Tommasini and the historical commentary on *The Prince* by the British scholar Lawrence Arthur Burd), no other period has probably had such a limited vision of the ex-Florentine secretary.

The influence of the French Revolution (and Hegel) on Machiavelli studies reached well into the twentieth century, especially in Italy and Germany. In the aftermath of World War I (1914–1918), a defeated Germany embarked on a series of profound transformations. Once the Reich founded by Chancellor Otto von Bismarck in 1871 was abolished, the republic was proclaimed, but attempts to cut ties with the past, in particular by demilitarizing Prussian society, met with strong resistance, fueling a fiery conflict between the nostalgic and the innovators. At that time, for more than a century, Germany had been Europe's philosophical beating heart, as well as the country where new historical investigation based on archival research and modern philology took shape. It is not surprising, therefore, that the unprecedented postwar situation bore special fruit in such an intellectually vibrant environment.

This is also true for Machiavelli studies. In the light of the defeat of Prussia's power politics, in a time of great insecurity and even despair, older scholars turned to *The Prince* to discuss the role of force in society and international relations. In 1919 the great sociologist Max Weber gave a lecture at the University of Munich on "Politics as a Vocation," and even if he never mentioned Machiavelli, the large audience (and later Weber's readers) assumed that the Florentine thinker was one of his first objects of concern. In a paper full of concepts already developed in previous works, Weber introduced here the original contrast between what he called "the ethics of conviction" (*Gesinnungsethik*) and "the ethics of responsibility" (*Verantwortungsethik*). Typical of religions and revolutionary movements, the former affirms that men must pay attention only to the goodness of their beliefs, without worrying too much about the potential consequences; the latter, on the contrary, invites them to weigh carefully the potential costs of each choice but also recognizes that in particular conditions violence may be inevitable in view of a greater good—just like *The Prince*.

The other great figure to approach Machiavelli was the eminent historian Friedrich Meinecke, the author of a voluminous monograph on *Machiavellism: The Doctrine of Raison d'État and Its Place in Modern History* (1924). Meinecke, too, was obsessed with the disastrous outcome of German aggression, and his grand narrative, which runs from Machiavelli to Bismarck, interprets modern European history through the contrast between an unbridled power politics and moralizing attempts to contain interstate struggles for supremacy. In Meinecke's view Machiavelli was a neopagan thinker (in a clear Burckhardtian key), and his anti-Christian stance was what enabled him to recover the ancients' reason-of-State theory and carry it to its extreme conclusions. Meinecke's work, however, had more than just historical aims: it was also designed to offer guidance for the present. As noted by some of the first reviewers, such as the German right-wing jurist Carl Schmitt and the Italian liberal-conservative philosopher Benedetto Croce, the whole book is grounded on a series of binary oppositions (*krátos* versus *éthos*; self-interest versus ethical norm; force versus law; empirical reality versus natural right; nature versus culture), and Meinecke evokes countless historical examples in order to express the hope that a synthesis may be finally achieved thanks to a moralized reason of State, ready to admit violence, deception, and treason only as exceptions to higher principles that must be preserved as much as possible.

Precisely because of the role played by *The Prince* in Hegel's theory of the state (and that of his followers, like the right-wing nationalist historian Heinrich von Treitschke, a close collaborator of Bismarck), German scholars interested in the recent history of their country had to come to terms with Machiavelli. It is no surprise, then, that in the same years this confrontation was particularly heated in Italy as well, that is, in the country where Hegel's idealism had borne its most original fruits outside of Germany. Everyday political struggles conditioned judgments chiefly in the aftermath of the March on Rome (1922), when Benito Mussolini had started to claim the great Florentine's legacy for himself with the essay "Prelude to Machiavelli" (April 1924) and to affirm the absolute primacy of the state over the citizens in a caricature of Hegel's thesis (as the historian and fascist minister Francesco Ercole would eventually do in a collection of essays fully reworked as *Machiavelli's Politics*, 1926). In this perspective, Machiavelli rapidly became fundamental to the fascist project that would abolish the individual rights inscribed in the 1848 liberal constitution and in the checks and balances of the parliamentary system. "Everything in the State, nothing outside the State, nothing against the State," as Mussolini would proclaim on the third anniversary of the March on Rome. By contrast, relaunching the thesis of the separation of politics from ethics (and not of the subordination of the latter to the former), as Croce did ("Machiavelli and Vico: Politics and Ethics," July 1924), was a way of preserving a space for the autonomy of individuals outside the fascist totalitarian "Ethical State" in the name of liberal rights and freedoms (even if, at that point, Croce still saw in Mussolini a providential instrument against socialism). But Croce was far from alone in his perplexity, and in the same tense context, in June, a leading antifascist, Piero Gobetti (who would die in 1926 at the age of twenty-six as a result of the Black Shirts' aggression), replied to Mussolini that Machiavelli was the thinker not (only) of the omnipotent state but also of popular rule, and easily demonstrated that in the *Discourses* Machiavelli had even praised social conflicts as an indispensable source of strength for the republic.

Mussolini's endorsement had a huge impact on Machiavelli's image and reputation in subsequent years, to the point that soon it became common for European intellectuals to read *The Prince* in order to understand what fascism was or to have a privileged key to Il Duce's mind; so, when in 1927 the four-hundredth anniversary of Machiavelli's death was celebrated worldwide in the newspapers, even outside of Italy writers and journalists could not avoid mentioning Mussolini (for instance, the great poet Thomas Sterling Eliot did so in the *Times Literary Supplement*). Yet totalitarian thinkers' enthusiasm for Machiavelli was not a foregone conclusion. For instance, the leading fascist intellectual Giovanni Gentile (minister of public educa-tion from 1922 to 1924 and coauthor with Mussolini of the offi-cial encyclopedic entry on "Fascism," among many other offi-cial positions) appreciated *The Prince* only partially, because, in his view, Machiavelli had failed to recognize fully the moral value of the state and could not go beyond an individualist approach to politics; for this reason, instead of him, in a confer-ence that was also a sort of benevolent, friendly reply to Mus-solini (October 1924), Gentile indicated the seventeenth-century friar and utopian political thinker Tommaso Campanella as the true inspirer of the regime for the great importance that he had given to religion in civic life, in a sort of synthesis of Machia-velli and Savonarola that had allowed Campanella to overcome the gap between the private and the public sphere, the individ-ual and the people, politics and ethics.

Likewise, the main German political philosopher under the Third Reich (1933–1945), Carl Schmitt, was skeptical about Machiavelli, before he changed his mind under Mussolini's influence. In his first works, Schmitt attacked *The Prince* for its (typically modern) "technical"/detached approach to politics (*The Dictatorship*, 1921) and for its lack of any religious transcendence. Later, however, endorsing Mussolini's sympathy for Machia-velli, Schmitt lauded the Florentine thinker's grasp of the fun-damentally conflictual nature of political relations (*Machiavelli*, 1927) and compared him favorably to Hobbes for not falling prey to the myth of a "technified" modern state (*The Leviathan in the State Theory of Thomas Hobbes*, 1938). But another adjustment happened after World War II, when Schmitt (now expelled from German universities for his Nazi past) accused Machiavelli of having spoken of the essence of power too openly and of having made visible to everybody (and therefore unleashed) its destructive force; politics, Schmitt argued, is above all mystery, and thus its covert procedures must be kept secret (*Glossarium*, written between 1947 and 1951 but posthumously published in 1991). In his eyes, therefore, Machiavelli's "illuminist" desire to show things "as they are" became retrospectively responsible for the massacres of the twentieth century. Schmitt therefore paradoxically reached the same conclusion as the many antifascist thinkers who in the 1930s and 1940s had reproached Machiavelli for being the truest inspirer of Mussolini's and Hitler's crimes—authors as disparate as the French Catholic theologian Jacques Maritain, the French liberal-conservative sociologist Raymond Aron, the German nationalist-conservative historian Gerhard Ritter, and the Italian socialist historian and antifascist émigré Gaetano Salvemini.

To synthesize the passionate debate on Machiavelli that was triggered in Western Europe by Mussolini's *Prelude* (and that continued even after the end of World War II), it is possible to classify the different positions into four major groups, according to the different figures' attitude toward Il Duce's 1924 claim that *The Prince* had announced fascism and to their overall judgment of Machiavelli (table 5.2).

Table 5.2. **Machiavelli and fascism**

	Pro-Machiavelli +	Anti-Machiavelli –
Protofascist Machiavelli +	*The Fascist Prophet* Mussolini, Ercole, Schmitt 1927, Schmitt 1938 + +	*A Friend of the Tyrants* Maritain, Aron, Ritter, Salvemini + –
Not protofascist Machiavelli –	*An Enemy of the Tyrants* Croce, Gobetti, Gramsci – +	*An Individualist Thinker* Gentile – –

The Soviet case is telling too. Machiavelli had been much studied in Russia since the end of the nineteenth century, and the Bolshevik leader Vladimir Lenin is believed to have known his writings well (even if he mentions him just once, in a 1922 letter: "One wise writer on matters of statecraft rightly said that if it was necessary to resort to certain brutalities for the sake of realizing a given political goal, they must be carried out in the most energetic fashion and in the briefest possible time because the masses will not tolerate prolonged application of brutality"). After the Socialist Revolution in 1917, many scholars continued working on Machiavelli and especially on his analysis of Florentine class struggles in order to corroborate with his examples Marx's materialist laws of history. Yet Machiavelli proved to be potentially relevant in more contemporary quarrels as well. For instance, when, after Lenin's death in 1924, his successor Joseph Stalin started concentrating all powers on himself, Vladimir Nikolaevich Maksimovski, a reputed historian, used *The Prince* indirectly to warn him (with scarce success) that "the *principe nuovo*'s power must be temporary" (*The Idea of Dictatorship in Machiavelli*, 1929). But it was a brief season because, under Stalin, intellectual life gradually became almost impossible in Russia, and even working on Machiavelli turned out to be dangerous. Thus, when in one of their meetings, a primary Soviet leader, Lev Kamenev, was prosecuted at Stalin's request for his alleged antirevolutionary activities, the fact that two years earlier he had written a short introduction to a new translation of Machiavelli was used against him to prove his immorality and contributed to his death sentence. From that moment on, Machiavelli studies almost disappeared in Russia.

In the Mirror of the Weimar Republic (1946–Today)

The so-called Weimar Republic (1919–1933) was soon weakened by the far-right opposition and finally overwhelmed by Adolf Hitler's supporters. Nevertheless, the ideas shaped in that brief season of dire uncertainty and high hopes were destined to leave a lasting trace in twentieth-century thought in the most diverse fields—Machiavelli studies included. Weber and Meinecke were born in the 1860s, and although they reached very different conclusions, they were both still interested in reflecting retrospectively on the deep imprint that Hegel's Machiavelli had left on German politics. The real novelty came instead from a new generation of scholars, born around the beginning of the century and called to deal with Germany's troubles in their formative years, although their intuitions would yield fruit only a couple of decades later, in other countries and even on another continent. Among these, one must first of all mention three of Meinecke's students: the young historians Hans Baron, Felix Gilbert, and Nicolai Rubinstein. Driven by a genuine commitment to Germany's recently acquired democratic institutions, all of them presented a consistently republican Machiavelli, and they contributed not just to a reevaluation of the *Discourses* after their partial nineteenth-century eclipse but also to the insertion of this work into the intellectual and political tradition characteristic of the free Italian communes: what Baron defined as *Bürgerhumanismus*, civic humanism, first in a 1925 review of Meinecke and then in a 1928 monograph on Leonardo Bruni. In their reading Machiavelli was therefore not to be celebrated as an isolated genius but as the apex of an entire civilization, where modern freedom had its roots.

All three of Meinecke's students were Jewish, and upon Hitler's rise to power in 1933 they were forced to emigrate (like, among the Machiavelli scholars already mentioned, Cassirer and Hirschman). After countless difficulties, Baron and Gilbert settled in the United States and Rubinstein in England. Here their interest in the communes' political experience found fertile ground in the tradition of British and American liberalism, which since the nineteenth century had hailed medieval Italian city-states as a link between classical republicanism and modern liberty (to quote the British Romantic poet Percy Bysshe Shelley about the many wanderings of the same "flag of Freedom": "From age to age, from man to man, / It lived; and lit from land to land / Florence, Albion, Switzerland," *Hellas*, 1822). Reformulated in English, Baron's, Gilbert's, and Rubinstein's theses quickly spread throughout the world, promoting a rediscovery of the *Discourses* that constitutes the principal characteristic of Machiavelli studies in the second half of the twentieth century. (This major shift was announced by the first serious historical commentary on the work, which was produced in the United States by the Jesuit scholar Leslie J. Walker in 1950.) The two major English-language attempts to insert Machiavelli into a grand multisecular narrative—namely, John G. A. Pocock's *The Machiavellian Moment* (1975), which follows the fortunes of Florentine republicanism up to the English and American Revolutions, and the first volume of Quentin Skinner's *The Foundations of Modern Political Thought* (1978), which focuses on the language of politics in Italy from the thirteenth to the sixteenth centuries—would be unimaginable without the accomplishments of the German émigrés. Baron's *The Crisis of the Early Italian Renaissance* (1954), where the fifteenth-century wars between Florence and the dukes of Milan are explicitly retold in the light of the struggle of the Allies against Nazi Germany, and Gilbert's more nuanced *Machiavelli and Guicciardini* (1965) were especially relevant in this regard.

The influence of Weimar's cultural and political fights can also be appreciated in another type of interpretation, one that presents Machiavelli primarily as a liquidator of classical political philosophy—a position contrary to Pocock and Skinner, who instead insist on the continuity between ancient and modern republicanism even when they praise the *Discourses'* originality and relevance for our times. These readings also stem from some German thinkers who moved to America to escape Nazi persecution: the conservative philosophers Eric Voegelin and Leo Strauss and the theorist of civic engagement Hannah Arendt (the latter two also Jews). These three figures are very distant from one another and in some ways even politically antithetical; nonetheless, all three revived the anti-Machiavellian tradition in a grand narrative in which modernity no longer corresponds to the dialectically inevitable triumph of a progressive movement of spiritual enrichment, as in Hegel and nineteenth-century liberalism, but to a painful fall from the lost summit of Greek philosophy. Such an antimodern stance was probably a legacy of Martin Heidegger, by whose teaching both Strauss and Arendt were deeply influenced in their youth, although at that time Heidegger was a convinced Nazi supporter. Not by chance, another early admirer of Heidegger who was persecuted for his ideas under Hitler, the German political thinker Dolf Sternberger, would also express similar positions later in his life, in his 1978 book *Three Roots of Politics*.

In particular, for Strauss, Machiavelli is responsible for having substituted the fear of punishment for education, necessity for freedom, and the government of masses for the government of knowledgeable men—all by rejecting the great Socratic tradition of Plato, Aristotle, and Xenophon—even if here and there Strauss does not exclude the possibility that Machiavelli's writings can hide a secret teaching that runs counter to the most apparent one and is only accessible to the wise few (*Thoughts on Machiavelli*, 1958). As a part of the same rebuttal, in the name of natural right Strauss condemned the twentieth-century Austrian jurist Hans Kelsen's legal positivism (the intellectual tradition that emphasizes the conventional nature of law and that does not ground it on divine commandment, reason, or human rights) as a dangerous updating of Machiavelli's claims about the unlimited power of rulers (*Natural Right and History*, 1953).

Compared to Strauss's close readings, the interpretation proposed by Arendt in the same years relies on more superficial knowledge of *The Prince* and the *Discourses*. In the footpaths of Burckhardt, Arendt saw Machiavelli as a sort of Renaissance neopagan precursor of Nietzsche, fascinated by a worldly glory that is somehow beyond good and evil (because "badness can no more shine in glory than goodness," as she puts it in *The Human Condition*, 1958) and eager to overcome the ancient philosophers' wisdom by reversing Socrates's instruction "Be as you would wish to appear to others" into "Appear as you may wish to be" (*On Revolution*, 1963). At the same time, however, Machiavelli was much more than that. For Arendt, with his *Prince* he announced the characteristically modern trust in starting over from scratch. "He was the first to think about the possibility of founding a permanent, lasting, enduring body politics," she writes, and "the first to visualize the rise of a purely secular realm whose laws and principles of action were independent of the teaching of the Church"; for this reason, "one may well see in him the spiritual father of revolution." Despite Arendt's dislike for the French revolutionaries, who owed so much to Machiavelli, the simple fact that his lesson was decisive for the American Founding Fathers too in the end made him, at least partially, a positive figure for her.

After World War II (1939–1945), in the United States and Great Britain interest gradually shifted to the *Discourses*, and Machiavelli even became part and parcel of the Cold War propaganda against the Soviet Union about the origins of liberal values and institutions in the so-called Free World (at the risk of banalizing and sanitizing his thought). Quite to the contrary, in continental Europe there was greater hesitation in reclaiming Machiavelli's legacy, after decades in which the various forms of fascism had presented him as the theorist of power politics (symbolically, in 1936, to seal their friendship, Mussolini and Hitler exchanged editions of the complete works of Machiavelli and Nietzsche as gifts). So, even in Italy, where in the 1920s and 1930s political philosophers and politicians had squabbled over the meaning of *The Prince*, it was instead historical and philological studies on Machiavelli that flourished in the second half of the century (particularly relevant was the 1961 discovery that Machiavelli had transcribed Lucretius's *De rerum natura* in his youth, while, among the books published after 1945, at least the collections of essays by Federico Chabod and Carlo Dionisotti deserve mention for their importance).

A notable exception arises with the Marxist theorists. One of the great twentieth-century interpretations of Machiavelli is

certainly the one proposed by Antonio Gramsci, the secretary
of the Italian Communist Party, who was arrested by Mussolini's regime at the end of 1926 as part of a systematic repression
of his opponents. From that moment on, Gramsci (who as a
young man, before devoting himself to politics, had been a
promising linguist) spent the rest of his life in custody, and here,
as far as he was allowed by the strict prison regulations, he
resumed his studies, trying to investigate the remote causes of
socialism's defeat in Italy. Among the books he read with the
greatest care was Machiavelli's *The Prince*—a work that he interpreted as a sort of manual for the revolutionary takeover to be
adopted by what Gramsci called the "modern prince," namely,
the new mass political party. As a result, some of the ideas for
which Gramsci is famous today were born out of his dialogue
with Machiavelli: from the positive evaluation of political myth
as an instrument of persuasion that structures abstract thought
in memorable images, to the need to involve the rural countryside in urban political struggles through military conscription,
up to the contrast between a "war of position" and a "war of
maneuver" during a revolutionary fight (an idea that Gramsci
drew from the antithesis between the feudal organization of the
Kingdom of France and the centralized government of the Ottoman Empire in chapter 4 of *The Prince*).

Published posthumously between 1948 and 1951, *The Prison
Notebooks* soon became a point of reference for Italian culture
and, later, a worldwide twentieth-century classic. It was precisely
Gramsci's references to *The Prince* that nourished the interest in
Machiavelli of the socialist and communist left at a time when
many readers continued to view him with suspicion. In France
and Italy, for example, since the 1960s at least four important

Marxist/radical philosophers have worked on Machiavelli: Claude Lefort, Louis Althusser, Roberto Esposito, and Toni Negri (and the American political theorist Neal Wood could be added to this list). Lefort, especially, invested considerable energy in interpreting *The Prince* and the *Discourses* in a voluminous doctoral thesis later published in 1972 as *Machiavelli in the Making*. Coming from the anti-Stalinist and libertarian Marxist left, which had become especially vocal after the youth protest movements of May 1968, Lefort had turned to Machiavelli as an alternative to the Soviet model, endorsing above all his appreciation for Rome's well-regulated conflicts. In his eyes, the *Discourses* confirmed that it was not only impossible to eliminate the fractures of the social body but also undesirable to do so (a thesis formulated in a direct polemic against Soviet representations of Russia after 1917 as a classless state). The same Machiavelli whom many continued to present as a friend of tyrants and a theorist of absolutism (if not autocracy) came in Lefort's pages to offer the best antidote to totalitarianism, with the result that rather than announcing modern politics (as in so many nineteenth- and twentieth-century interpretations), his Machiavelli is invoked as, if anything, a possible therapy for its most evident distortions.

This new approach characterizes many late twentieth-century readings of Machiavelli, and it is likely the result of a more disillusioned attitude toward modernity that can be associated with the almost simultaneous rise of the concept of "postmodernism" (very fashionable in the 1980s and 1990s). This profound shift is especially evident in the evolution of Skinner's reading. While in his *Foundations of Modern Political Thought* he was still trying to reconstruct a genealogy of the modern state (in very Hegelian terms), in his later studies (such as *Liberty Before Liberalism*, 1998, which was deeply inspired by Philip Pettit's *Republicanism: A Theory of Freedom and Government*, 1997), Skinner became instead the champion of a disregarded neo-Roman (and Machiavellian) conception of freedom as an alternative to both Greek and contemporary (that is, liberal) ones. Scholars usually distinguish "positive liberty" (or liberty *to*), the freedom to act and to be involved in public life, and "negative liberty" (or liberty *from*), the absence of external obstacles and constraints, and they associate them respectively to the ancients and the moderns. In the 1990s Pettit and Skinner, however, argued that there is a third way of conceiving freedom: the Roman and Machiavellian way—a unique form of "negative liberty" (like the moderns'), which highly values civic participation (like the Greeks'), but just in order to preserve one's own condition of nondomination (as a means, therefore, and not as a goal in itself). Somehow, according to them (and contrary to contemporary liberalism), "negative liberty" is always imperiled, and for this reason it has to be constantly defended in the public arena—as the *Discourses* taught in an exemplary fashion. Like Lefort, therefore, for Pettit and Skinner too Machiavelli becomes relevant to our time not as the father of our modernity but for the many forgotten lessons that we should recover from him in a time of dangerous democratic apathy.

Different still is the reading of Machiavelli proposed by the French philosopher Michel Foucault in his 1978 course on *Security, Territory, Population* (published posthumously only in 2004). Founding his interpretation just on *The Prince* (and ignoring the *Discourses'* positive judgment of the people as an autonomous political actor), Foucault focused his narrative on the sixteenth-century evolution of the instruments of control and saw in Machiavelli the peak of medieval political theory rather than the inaugurator of modern thought. In his view, while Machiavelli was still preoccupied only with the defense of the ruler's security and territory, the decisive break occurred later, with late sixteenth- and seventeenth-century authors who started focusing on the well-being of the whole population instead and, in doing so, gave birth to what Foucault calls "governmentality": a new "art of government" that includes a wide range of disciplining techniques and takes special care of the subjects' needs and desires in order to secure their consensus. For Foucault, therefore, Machiavelli is neither modern nor especially relevant for our (highly regulated, even if invisibly) present world but just a minor figure in his all-encompassing grand narrative.

The principal nineteenth- and twentieth-century readings of Machiavelli could also therefore be easily classed into four major families (table 5.3), this time according to his position in the history of Western political thought and the suitability of his teachings for us today (the considerable differences clearly depend in this case also on the many ways in which the elusive category of "modernity" is employed and when it starts—the Renaissance? the Enlightenment? modern liberalism?).

And today? After the end of the Cold War (1947–1991) and the dissolution of the Soviet Union (1991), in a period certainly not lacking in planetary shocks (the terrorist attack on the Twin Towers in 2001 and the U.S. invasion of Afghanistan and Iraq, the economic crisis in 2008, the advance of populist and far-right movements, the COVID pandemic in 2020, the Ukrainian war in 2022), no public event has had an impact on Machiavelli studies comparable to the French Revolution and the birth of the

Table 5.3. Machiavelli and us

	Suitable +	Not suitable –
Modern Machiavelli +	*The Founder* Machiavelli as the father of scientific politics, political realism, the modern state, modern constitutionalism, the autonomy of politics, revolution, etc. (Hegel, Wolff, Burckhardt, Meinecke, Mussolini, Croce, Gramsci, Gilbert, Cassirer, Arendt 1963, Pocock, Skinner 1978) + +	*The Corrupter* Machiavelli as the advocate of irreligious politics (Mazères and the other adversaries of the French Revolution), as the embodiment of "technified" politics (Schmitt 1921), or as the destroyer of ancient wisdom (Strauss, Arendt 1958, Voegelin) + –
Premodern Machiavelli –	*The Forgotten Master* Machiavelli as a rare expert of the true warring essence of politics (Schmitt 1938), as the theoretician of never-ending conflicts (Lefort), or as the promoter of neo-Roman liberty (Pettit, Skinner 1998) – +	*The Ancestor* Machiavelli as a prescientific thinker (Mosca) or as the culmination of the medieval art of government (Foucault) – –

Weimar Republic, but research on his life and works continues to flourish. Beyond the many discoveries made by historians and philologists, a new overall reading of *The Prince* and the *Discourses* has begun to take shape, especially since 2011. People speak of a "plebeian" or "democratic turn" because, on both sides of the Atlantic, a recent wave of scholars has increasingly drawn attention to the antioligarchic core of Machiavelli's thought: his persistent hostility to the Florentine "mighty," his confidence in ordinary citizens' self-governance, his approval of a class institution such as the tribunes of the plebs to counter the Senate, his sensitivity to the issue of public debt as a means for the Florentine financial oligarchy to enrich itself at the expense of the whole community (and to the ways of getting rid of that debt through popular conscription), and the lasting legacy of his positive assessment of social conflict in Western political thought. With some simplification, one could say that in the last years scholars started appreciating Machiavelli precisely for his original rejection of classical republicanism's pro-oligarchic leaning, to the point that their Machiavelli somehow resembles Guicciardini's, but with the notable difference that, instead of shunning the *Discourses'* pro-popular stance, now they fully endorse it. In this light, the plebeian/democratic interpreters of Machiavelli strongly believe in the preciousness of his teachings for fighting the social inequalities of the twentieth-first century: for them, too, he is a "forgotten master" who can help us amend the injustices of our present.

This new interpretation cannot be traced back to any of the three currents that monopolized debate in the second half of the twentieth century—the Marxists, the neorepublicans, and the Straussians—although it has several traits in common with each of them. With the Marxists it shares the idea that Machiavelli was a radical political thinker, but, compared to them, it is much more interested in the institutional creativity of the *Discourses*. From the so-called Cambridge School of Pocock, Skinner, and Pettit it takes up the conviction that Machiavelli never denied his youthful ideals of liberty, while rejecting the existence of a single republican tradition and insisting on the huge distance between the pro-popular *Discourses* and pro-aristocratic authors such as Cicero, Bruni, Guicciardini, or Montesquieu. It is close to the reading of Strauss's disciples in the idea that, by siding with the people, Machiavelli broke with classical and humanistic political thought, but it does not accept Strauss's condemnation of Machiavelli as a corrupter of the wisdom of the ancients. The blend of these elements, however, is entirely new—not least because it rests largely on an appreciation of previously over-looked passages from *The Prince* and the *Discourses* (starting with Machiavelli's attention to economic factors, his approval of Rome's openness toward newcomers and defeated enemies, and his insistence on the importance of the tribunes of the plebs in the Roman mixed constitution).

The story, of course, does not end here: more Machiavellis will come—as this is the prerogative of true classics. However, amid a thousand condemnations and an equal number of redis-coveries, at least one undisputable development has happened in the last five centuries. Machiavelli became one of the "ancient men," the few guides to whom one always turns in search of inspiration and comfort, of whom he speaks with moving words in his famous December 10, 1513, letter to Vettori about the com-position of *The Prince*:

When the evening has come, I go back home, and I enter my office; and at the door I take off that daily dress, full of mud and dirt, and I put on royal and curial clothes; and dressed up I enter in the ancient courts of the ancient men, where, benev-olently received by them, I eat that food that is only mine, and for which I was born; where I am not ashamed to speak to them, and to ask them the reason for their actions; and they respond to me out of their humanity; and for four hours I feel no annoyance, I forget all anxieties, I do not fear poverty, I am not dismayed by death: I put my whole self into them.

It is easy to suppose that Machiavelli will accompany us for a long time, in this new millennium too.

Chronology

1469	Niccolò Machiavelli's birth. Upon his father Piero's death, Lorenzo de' Medici, later known as the Magnificent, becomes informal lord of Florence.
1472	The art of typography is introduced in Florence.
1478	Giuliano, brother of Lorenzo, is killed in the failed Pazzi conspiracy against the Medici.
1480	The oligarchic Council of the Seventy is established in Florence.
1492	Death of Lorenzo de' Medici, who is succeeded informally by his son Piero. Rodrigo Borgia is elected pope as Alexander VI. Christopher Columbus reaches America.
1494	Expedition in Italy of the king of France Charles VIII to conquer Naples. Rebellion of Pisa, exile of the Medici, and institution of the Great Council at the suggestion of the friar Girolamo Savonarola.
1495	French retreat and battle against the Italians at Fornovo.
1498	Trial and execution of Savonarola for heresy. Machiavelli is elected to the chancery.
1499	The new king of France, Louis XII, occupies Milan.

1499–1503	With the help of his father, Alexander VI, Cesare Borgia builds the Duchy of Romagna.
1501	France and Spain conquer the Kingdom of Naples.
1502	Piero Soderini is elected standardbearer of justice for life in Florence.
1503	Giuliano della Rovere is elected pope as Julius II. Cesare Borgia loses all his possessions (which are occupied by the Venetians).
1504	The entire Kingdom of Naples passes to Spain after a war with France.
1506	The Florentine militia's first parade. Julius II reconquers Perugia and Bologna.
1509	Venice is defeated by the League of Cambrai arranged by Julius II (Papal States, Holy Roman Empire, France, and Spain) at Agnadello. Julius II reconquers the Romagna. Florence reconquers Pisa.
1512	The French defeat the Holy League arranged by Julius II (Papal States, Holy Roman Empire, Spain, England, and Venice) at Ravenna, but they have to leave Italy all the same. Sack of Prato by the Spaniards and oligarchic coup, which brings the Medici back to Florence. Machiavelli's dismissal from the chancery.
1513	Conspiracy against the Medici in Florence: Machiavelli is imprisoned and tortured. Cardinal Giovanni de' Medici, son of Lorenzo the Magnificent, is elected pope as Leo X, and Lorenzo di Piero de' Medici becomes informal lord of Florence. Abolition of the Great Council. Composition of *The Prince*.

Reconstitution of the oligarchic Council of the Seventy.

1515   The new king of France, Francis I, takes Milan back.

1515–1516   Machiavelli begins to attend the meetings of the Rucellai Gardens.

1516   Lorenzo de' Medici is made duke of Urbino by Leo X.

1517   Martin Luther affixes the Ninety-Five Theses in Wittenberg.

1517–1518   The present of the *Discourses on Livy*.

1519   The new king of Spain, Charles I, is elected emperor as Charles V. Lorenzo, son of Piero de' Medici, dies.

1520   The University of Pisa commissions the *Florentine Histories*. First representation of *The Mandrake*.

1521   *The Art of War* is printed in Florence. Death of Leo X. Machiavelli writes the *Discursus Florentinarum rerum* at the request of Cardinal Giulio de' Medici, cousin of Leo X.

1522   The French are definitively expelled from Milan. A conspiracy against Cardinal Giulio, organized by some of Machiavelli's friends from the Rucellai Gardens, is discovered (but this time Machiavelli is not suspected).

1523   Cardinal Giulio is elected pope as Clement VII. Agostino Nifo publishes the *De regnandi peritia* in Naples.

1525   The *Florentine Histories* are offered to Clement VII. Francis I is taken prisoner by Charles V's army at Pavia.

1526   Francis I is freed. League of Cognac (France, Papal States, Florence, Milan, and Genoa) against Charles V. Machiavelli works for the league under his friend Francesco Guicciardini. Nifo attacks Machiavelli again from Naples in his *De rege et tyranno.*

1527   Sack of Rome by Charles V's army and new expulsion of the Medici from Florence. Abolition of the Counsel of the Seventy and reconstitution of the Great Council. Machiavelli's failed attempt to recover his old place in chancery. Machiavelli dies.

1530   Guicciardini composes the *Considerations on the "Discourses."* Formal coronation of Charles V as emperor by Clement VII. Definitive return of the Medici to Florence with Charles V's military support.

1531   First printed edition of the *Discourses* (in Rome and Florence).

1532   First printed edition of *The Prince* and the *Florentine Histories* (in Rome and Florence).

1539   Reginald Pole writes the *Apologia ad Carolum V.*

1559   Machiavelli's works are included in the first *Index of Prohibited Books.*

1573   Giuliano de' Ricci, Machiavelli's grandson, copies several unpublished works of his ancestor, preserving them for posterity.

Further Readings

All translations in the book (from Latin, Italian, French, and German) are mine; ancient Greek texts are brought into English from the fifteenth-century Latin versions accessible to Machiavelli (but such humanistic adaptations were always also checked against the Greek originals).

Given the vast bibliography on Machiavelli, just a few suggestions can be made here; as a result, only articles especially relevant to my interpretation are listed. The titles that are already mentioned in full in the last chapter on Machiavelli's legacy are not repeated in the bibliography. Special attention has been given to recent works accessible in English.

Editions

Machiavelli, Niccolò. *Opere.* 3 vols. Ed. C. Vivanti. Torino: Einaudi, 1997–2005.

Machiavelli, Niccolò. *The Prince.* Ed. W. Connell. New York: Macmillan, 2016.

Machiavelli, Niccolò. *Il Principe. Nuova edizione annotata.* Ed. G. Pedullà. Rome: Donzelli, 2022.

Machiavelli, Niccolò. *The Prince*. Ed. G. Pedullà. Trans. P. Gaborik. London: Verso, forthcoming.

Machiavelli, Niccolò. *The Discourses on Livy*. In *The Sweetness of Power: Machiavelli's "Discourses" & Guicciardini's "Considerations."* Ed. J. B. Atkinson and D. Sices. DeKalb: Northern Illinois University Press, 2002.

Machiavelli, Niccolò. *The Art of War*. Ed. N. Wood. Trans. E. Farneworth. Rev. ed. Boston: Da Capo, 2001.

Machiavelli, Niccolò. *The Comedies of Machiavelli*. Ed. J. B. Atkinson and D. Sices. Indianapolis, IN: Hackett, 2007.

Machiavelli, Niccolò. *The Florentine Histories*. Ed. L. F. Banfield and H. C. Mansfield. Princeton, NJ: Princeton University Press, 1988.

Recently Attributed Works

Conti, Daniele. *I "quadernucci" di Niccolò Machiavelli. Frammenti storici Palatini*. Pisa: Edizioni della Normale, 2023.

Landon, William J. *Filippo Strozzi and Niccolò Machiavelli: Patron, Client, and the "Pistola della peste."* Toronto: Toronto University Press, 2013.

Machiavelli, Niccolò. *Commedia in versi*. Ed. P. Stoppelli. Roma: Edizioni di Storia e Letteratura, 2018.

Machiavelli, Niccolò. *Epistola della peste*. Ed. P. Stoppelli. Roma: Edizioni di Storia e Letteratura, 2019.

Reference Works on Machiavelli

Cutinelli-Rendina, Emanuele. "Niccolò Machiavelli (Firenze 1469–1527)." In *Autografi dei letterati italiani. Il Cinquecento*. 3 vols. of announced 5. Ed. M. Motolese, P. Procaccioli, and E. Russo, 1:271–83. Rome: Salerno, 2009–.

Dunn, John, and Ian Harris, eds. *Great Political Thinkers: Machiavelli*. 2 vols. Cheltenham: Elgar, 1997.

Innocenti, Piero, and Marielisa Rossi, eds. *Bibliografia delle edizioni di Niccolò Machiavelli*. 4 vols. Manziana: Vecchiarelli, 2015–2023.

Sasso, Gennaro, and Giorgio Inglese, eds. *Enciclopedia Machiavelliana*. Rome: Treccani, 2014. https://www.treccani.it/enciclopedia/elenco -opere/Enciclopedia_machiavelliana.

Historical Context

von Albertini, Rudolf. *Das Florentinische Staatsbewusstsein im Übergang von der Republik zum Prinzipat*. Bern: Francke, 1955.

Aubert, Alberto. *La crisi degli antichi stati italiani (1492–1521)*. Firenze: Le Lettere, 2003.

Braudel, Fernand. *Out of Italy: Two Centuries of World Domination and Demise*. 1973. New York: Europa Editions, 2019.

Brown, Alison. *Piero di Lorenzo de' Medici and the Crisis of Renaissance Italy*. Cambridge: Cambridge University Press, 2020.

Gamberini, Andrea, and Isabella Lazzarini, eds. *The Italian Renaissance State (1350–1520)*. Cambridge: Cambridge University Press, 2012.

Mallet, Michael, and Christine Shaw. *The Italian Wars (1494–1559): War, State, and Society in Early Modern Europe*. New York: Routledge, 2012.

Najemy, John M., ed. *Italy in the Age of the Renaissance (1300–1550)*. Oxford: Oxford University Press, 2004.

Najemy, John M. *A History of Florence (1200–1575)*. Malden, MA: Blackwell, 2006.

Tewes, Götz-Rüdiger. *Kampf um Florenz: Die Medici im Exil (1494–1512)*. Cologne: Böhlau, 2011.

Trexler, Richard C. *Public Life in Renaissance Florence*. Ithaca, NY: Cornell University Press, 1980.

Cultural Context

Brown, Alison. *Bartolomeo Scala, 1430–1497, Chancellor of Florence: The Humanist as Bureaucrat*. Princeton, NJ: Princeton University Press, 1979.

Brown, Alison. *The Return of Lucretius to Renaissance Florence*. Cambridge, MA: Harvard University Press, 2010.

Buttay-Jutier, Florence. *"Fortuna." Usages politiques d'une allégorie morale à la Renaissance*. Paris: Presses de l'Université Paris-Sorbonne, 2008.

Cappelli, Guido. *L'umanesimo italiano da Petrarca a Valla*. Roma: Carocci, 2010.

Chiodo, Domenico, and Rossana Sodano. *Le Muse sedizione. Un volto ignorato del petrarchismo*. Milan: FrancoAngeli, 2012.

Comanducci, Rita Maria. "Gli Orti Oricellari." *Interpres* 15 (1995–1996): 302–58.

Hankins, James, ed. *The Cambridge Companion to Renaissance Philosophy*. Cambridge: Cambridge University Press, 2007.

Kraye, Jill, ed. *The Cambridge Companion to Renaissance Humanism*. Cambridge: Cambridge University Press, 1996.

Luzzatto, Sergio, and Gabriele Pedullà, eds. *Atlante della letteratura italiana*. 3 vols. Torino: Einaudi, 2010–2012.

Rico, Francisco. *El sueño del humanismo*. Rev. ed. Barcelona: Destino, 2002.

Witt, Ronald G. *In the Footsteps of the Ancients: The Origins of Humanism from Lovato to Bruni*. Leiden: Brill, 2000.

Wyatt, Michael, ed. *The Cambridge Companion to the Italian Renaissance*. Cambridge: Cambridge University Press, 2014.

Renaissance Political Thought and Historiography

Cappelli, Guido. *"Maiestas." Politica e pensiero politico nella Napoli aragonese (1443–1503)*. Roma: Carocci, 2016.

Celati, Marta. *Conspiracy Literature in Early Renaissance Italy: Historiography and Princely Ideology*. Oxford: Oxford University Press, 2020.

Coleman, Janet. *A History of Political Thought: From the Middle Ages to the Renaissance*. Malden, MA: Blackwell, 2000.

Gilbert, Felix. "Florentine Political Assumptions in the Period of Savonarola and Soderini." *Journal of the Warburg and Courtauld Institutes* 20, nos. 3–4 (1957): 187–214.

Hankins, James. *Virtue Politics: Soulcraft and Statecraft in Renaissance Italy.* Cambridge, MA: Belknap, 2019.

Ianziti, Gary. *Writing History in Renaissance Italy: Leonardo Bruni and the Uses of the Past.* Cambridge, MA: Harvard University Press, 2012.

Pedullà, Gabriele. "Giro d'Europa. Le mille vite di Dionigi di Alicarnasso (XV–XIX secolo)." In Dionigi di Alicarnasso, *Storia di Roma antica*, ed. F. Donadi and G. Pedullà, lix–clix. Torino: Einaudi, 2010.

Pedullà, Gabriele. "Humanist Republicanism: Towards a New Paradigm." *History of Political Thought* 41, no. 1 (2020): 43–95.

Pedullà, Gabriele. "Athenian Democracy in Late Middle Ages and Early Humanism" and "Athenian Democracy in the Italian Renaissance." In *Companion to the Reception of Athenian Democracy*, ed. D. Piovan and G. Giorgini, 57–152. Leiden: Brill, 2020.

Pedullà, Gabriele. "Scipio vs. Caesar: The Poggio-Guarino Debate Without Republicanism." In *Republicanism: A Theoretical and Historical Perspective*, ed. M. Fantoni and F. Ricciardelli, 275–305. Roma: Viella, 2020.

Quondam, Amedeo. *Forma del vivere. L'etica del gentiluomo e i moralisti italiani.* Bologna: Il Mulino, 2010.

Shaw, Christine. *Reason and Experience in Renaissance Italy.* Cambridge: Cambridge University Press, 2021.

Viroli, Maurizio. *From Politics to Reason of State: The Acquisition and Transformation of the Language of Politics (1250–1600).* Cambridge: Cambridge University Press, 1992.

Wilcox, Donald J. *The Development of Florentine Humanist Historiography in the Fifteenth Century.* Cambridge, MA: Harvard University Press, 1969.

General Overviews of Machiavelli's Life and Work

Celenza, Christopher C. *Machiavelli: A Portrait.* Cambridge, MA: Harvard University Press, 2015.

Del Lucchese, Filippo. *The Political Philosophy of Machiavelli*. Edinburgh: Edinburgh University Press, 2015.

Fournel, Jean-Louis, and Jean-Claude Zancarini. *Machiavel: une vie en guerres*. Paris: Passés composés, 2020.

Lee, Alexander. *Machiavelli: His Life and Times*. London: Picador, 2020.

Najemy, John M. *Machiavelli's Broken World*. Oxford: Oxford University Press, 2022.

Skinner, Quentin. *Machiavelli: A Very Short Introduction*. Oxford: Oxford University Press, 1980. Rev. ed., 2019.

Vivanti, Corrado. *Niccolò Machiavelli: An Intellectual Biography*. Princeton, NJ: Princeton University Press, 2013. Italian original ed. 2008.

Zuckert, Catherine H. *Machiavelli's Politics*. Chicago: University of Chicago Press, 2017.

Collections of Essays on Machiavelli

Chabod, Federico. *Machiavelli and the Renaissance*. Cambridge, MA: Harvard University Press, 1959.

Connell, William. *Machiavelli nel Rinascimento italiano*. Milano: FrancoAngeli, 2015.

Dionisotti, Carlo. *Machiavellerie. Storia e fortuna di Machiavelli*. Torino: Einaudi, 1980.

Esposito, Roberto. *Ordine e conflitto. Machiavelli e la letteratura politica del Rinascimento italiano*. Napoli: Liguori, 1984.

Gilbert, Felix. *History: Choice and Commitment*. Cambridge, MA: Belknap, 1977.

Ginzburg, Carlo. *Nevertheless: Machiavelli, Pascal*. London: Verso, 2022. Italian original ed. 2018.

Mansfield, Harvey C. *Machiavelli's Virtue*. Chicago: University of Chicago Press, 1996.

Raimondi, Ezio. *Politica e commedia. Il centauro disarmato*. Rev. ed. Bologna: Il Mulino, 1998.

Sasso, Gennaro. *Machiavelli e gli antichi e altri saggi*. 4 vols. Milano-Napoli: Ricciardi, 1987–1997.

Multiauthored Volumes on Machiavelli

Ascoli, Albert R., and Victoria Kahn, eds. *Machiavelli and the Discourse of Literature*. Ithaca, NY: Cornell University Press, 1993.

Bock, Gisela, Quentin Skinner, and Maurizio Viroli, eds. *Machiavelli and Republicanism*. Cambridge: Cambridge University Press, 1993.

Del Lucchese, Filippo, Fabio Frosini, and Vittorio Morfino, eds. *The Radical Machiavelli*. Leiden: Brill, 2015.

Johnston, David C., Nadia Urbinati, and Camila Vergara Gonzalez, eds. *Machiavelli on Liberty and Conflict*. Chicago: University of Chicago Press, 2017.

Najemy, John M., ed. *Cambridge Companion to Machiavelli*. Cambridge: Cambridge University Press, 2010.

Pirés Aurélio, Diogo, and Andre Santos Campos, eds. *Machiavelli's "Discourses on Livy": A Critical Guide*. Leiden: Brill, 2021.

On Machiavelli's Family, Education, and Service in the Chancery

Black, Robert. *Machiavelli*. London: Routledge, 2013.

Boschetto, Luca. "'Uno uomo di basso e infimo stato'. Ricerche sulla storia familiare di Niccolò Machiavelli." *Archivio Storico Italiano* 176, no. 657 (2018): 485–524.

Godman, Peter. *From Poliziano to Machiavelli: Florentine Humanism in the High Renaissance*. Princeton, NJ: Princeton University Press, 1998.

Guidi, Andrea. *Un segretario militante. Politica, diplomazia e armi nel cancelliere Machiavelli*. Bologna: Il Mulino, 2009.

Marchand, Jean-Jacques. *Niccolò Machiavelli: i primi scritti politici (1499–1512). Nascita di un pensiero e di uno stile*. Padova: Antenore, 1975.

On *The Prince* and the *Discourses on Livy*

Althusser, Louis. *Machiavelli and Us.* London: Verso, 1999. French original ed. 1995.

Ardito, Alissa. *Machiavelli and the Modern State: "The Prince," the "Discourses on Livy," and the Extended Territorial Republic.* Cambridge: Cambridge University Press, 2015.

Barthas, Jérémie. *"L'argent n'est pas le nerf de la guerre." Essai sur une prétendue erreur de Machiavel.* Roma: École Française de Rome, 2011.

Barthas, Jérémie. "La composizione del 'Principe' di Machiavelli e la restaurazione dei Medici a Firenze. Per un nuovo paradigma interpretativo." *Rivista Storica Italiana* 131, no. 3 (2019): 761–811.

Mansfield, Harvey C. *Machiavelli's New Modes and Orders: A Study of the "Discourses on Livy."* Chicago: University of Chicago Press, 1979.

McCormick, John P. *Machiavellian Democracy.* Cambridge: Cambridge University Press, 2011.

Najemy, John M. *Between Friends: Discourses of Power and Desire in the Machiavelli-Vettori Letters of 1513–1515.* Princeton, NJ: Princeton University Press, 1993.

Pedullà, Gabriele. *Machiavelli in Tumult: The "Discourses on Livy" and the Origins of Political Conflictualism.* Cambridge: Cambridge University Press, 2018. Italian original ed. 2011.

Vatter, Miguel E. *Between Form and Event: Machiavelli's Theory of Political Freedom.* 2003. Berlin: Springer, 2010.

On the *Florentine Histories*

Clarke, Michelle T. *Machiavelli's Florentine Republic.* Cambridge: Cambridge University Press, 2018.

Jurdjevic, Mark. *A Great and Wretched City: Promise and Failure in Machiavelli's Florentine Political Thought.* Cambridge, MA: Harvard University Press, 2014.

Pedullà, Gabriele. "Il divieto di Platone. Niccolò Machiavelli e il discorso dell'anonimo plebeo ('Istorie Fiorentine' 3.13)." In *Storiografia repubblicana fiorentina*, eds. J.-J. Marchand and J.-C. Zancarini, 210–66. Firenze: Cesati, 2003.

Pedullà, Gabriele. "Una nuova fonte per il Ciompo: Niccolò Machiavelli e il 'De nobilitate' di Antonio de' Ferrariis." In *Renaissance Studies in Honor of Joseph Connors*, 2 vols., eds. M. Israëls and L.A. Waldman, II, 73–82. Milano: Officina Libraria, 2013.

Raimondi, Fabio. *Constituting Freedom: Machiavelli and Florence*. Oxford: Oxford University Press, 2018. Italian original ed. 2013.

On Machiavelli's Other Works

Erwin, Sean. *Machiavelli and the Problems of Military Force*. London: Bloomsbury Academic, 2022.

Guidi, Andrea. *Books, People, and Military Thought: Machiavelli's "Art of War" and the Fortune of the Militia in Sixteenth-Century Florence and Europe*. Leiden: Brill, 2020.

Stoppelli, Pasquale. *"La Mandragola": storia e filologia*. Roma: Bulzoni, 2005.

On Specific Topics

Benner, Erica. *Machiavelli's Ethics*. Princeton, NJ: Princeton University Press, 2010.

Berlin, Isaiah. "The Originality of Machiavelli." 1972. In *Against the Current: Essays in the History of Ideas*, 33–100. Princeton, NJ: Princeton University Press, 2013.

Campi, Alessandro. *Machiavelli and Political Conspiracies: The Struggle for Power in the Italian Renaissance*. New York: Routledge, 2018. Italian original ed. 2014.

Cappelli, Fredi. *Studi sul linguaggio del Machiavelli*. Firenze: Le Monnier, 1952.

Cutinelli-Rendina, Emanuele. *Chiesa e religione in Machiavelli*. Pisa: Istituti Editoriali e Poligrafici Internazionali, 1998.

De Caro, Mario. "Machiavelli's Lucretian View of Free Will." In *Lucretius: Poet and Philosopher: Background and Fortune of the "De rerum natura,"* ed. P. R. Hardie, V. Prosperi and D. Zucca, 205–21. Berlin: De Gruyter, 2020.

Evrigenis, Ioannis D. *Fear of Enemies and Collective Action*. Cambridge: Cambridge University Press, 2009.

Fenichel Pitkin, Hanna. *Fortune Is a Woman: Gender and Politics in the Thought of Niccolo Machiavelli*. Chicago: University of Chicago Press, 1984.

Gaille, Marie. *Machiavelli on Freedom and Civil Conflict: An Historical and Medical Approach*. Leiden: Brill, 2018. French original ed. 2004.

Hornqvist, Mikael. *Machiavelli and Empire*. Cambridge: Cambridge University Press, 2009.

Lettieri, Gaetano. "Nove tesi sull'ultimo Machiavelli." *Humanitas* 62, no. 5–6 (2017): 1034–89.

Nelson, Eric. *The Greek Tradition in Republican Thought*. Cambridge: Cambridge University Press, 2004.

Parel, Anthony J. *The Machiavellian Cosmos*. New Haven, CT: Yale University Press, 1992.

Stacey, Peter. *Roman Monarchy and the Renaissance Prince*. Cambridge: Cambridge University Press, 2007.

Winter, Yves. *Machiavelli and the Orders of Violence*. Cambridge: Cambridge University Press, 2018.

On Machiavelli's Reception

Anglo, Sidney. *Machiavelli: The First Century. Studies in Enthusiasm, Hostility, and Irrelevance*. Oxford: Oxford University Press, 2005.

Arienzo, Alessandro, and Alessandra Petrina eds. *Machiavellian Encounters in Tudor and Stuart England: Literary and Political Influences from the Reformation to the Restoration*. London: Routledge, 2013.

Barthas, Jérémie. "Machiavelli e i 'libertini' fiorentini (1522–1531). Una pagina dimenticata nella storia del libertinismo." *Rivista Storica Italiana* 120, no. 2 (2008): 569–603.

Ben Saad, Nizar. *Machiavel en France: des lumières à la Revolution*. Paris: L'Harmattan, 2007.

Carta, Paolo, and Xavier Tabet, eds. *Machiavelli nel XIX e XX secolo*. Trento: CEDAM, 2007.

Del Lucchese, Filippo. *Conflict, Power, and Multitude in Machiavelli and Spinoza: Tumult and Indignation*. London: Continuum, 2009. Italian original ed. 2004.

Figorilli, Cristina. *Lettori di Machiavelli tra Cinque e Seicento. Botero, Boccalini, Malvezzi*. Bologna: Patron, 2018.

Geuna, Marco. "Il linguaggio del repubblicanesimo di Adam Ferguson." In *I linguaggi politici delle rivoluzioni in Europa*, ed. E. Pii, 143–59. Firenze: Olschki, 1992.

Kahn, Victoria. *Machiavellian Rhetoric from the Counter-Reformation to Milton*. Princeton, NJ: Princeton University Press, 1994.

McCormick, John P. *Reading Machiavelli: Scandalous Books, Suspect Engagements, and the Virtue of Populist Politics*. Princeton, NJ: Princeton University Press, 2018.

Morfino, Vittorio. *The Spinoza-Machiavelli Encounter: Time and Occasion*. Edinburgh: Edinburgh University Press, 2018. Italian original ed. 2002.

Negri, Toni. *Insurgencies: Constituent Power and the Modern State*. Minneapolis: University of Minnesota Press, 1999. Italian original ed. 1992.

Pedullà, Gabriele. "Machiavelli dopo Auschwitz." In Felix Gilbert, *Machiavelli e Guicciardini*, ed. G. Pedullà, vii–xxxix. Torino: Einaudi, 2012.

Pedullà, Gabriele. "Aristotele *contra* Machiavelli. Il 'De regnandi peritia' di Agostino Nifo e la prima ricezione del 'Principe' nel Regno di Napoli." *L'Illuminista* 17, nos. 49–50–51 (2017): 295–350.

Pedullà, Gabriele. "Machiavelli secondo Carlo Ginzburg." *Storica* 24, no. 71 (2018): 9–86.

Pedullà, Gabriele. "Neal Wood e Machiavelli: ieri e oggi." *Almanacco di Filosofia e Politica* 3 (2021): 295–319.

Pedullà, Gabriele. "Il `De regnandi peritia' di Agostino Nifo: manifesto filosofico dei baroni napoletani." In *La crisi della modernità. Studi in onore di Gianvittorio Signorotto*, ed. M. Al Kalak, L. Ferrari, and E. Fumagalli, 407–25. Milan: FrancoAngeli, 2023.

Procacci, Giuliano. *Machiavelli nella cultura europea dell'età moderna.* 1965. Rev. ed. Roma-Bari: Laterza, 1995.

Rahe, Paul, ed. *Machiavelli's Liberal Republican Legacy.* Cambridge: Cambridge University Press, 2006.

Rees, E. A. *Political Thought from Machiavelli to Stalin: Revolutionary Machiavellism.* New York: Palgrave McMillan, 2004.

Ritter, Gerhard. *The Corrupting Influence of Power.* Essex: Tower Bridges, 1952. German original ed. 1940; rev. ed. 1947.

Sciara, Giuseppe. *Un'oscura presenza. Machiavelli nella cultura politica francese dal Termidoro alla Seconda Repubblica.* Roma: Edizioni di Storia e Letteratura, 2018.

Sullivan, Vickie B. *Machiavelli, Hobbes, and the Formation of a Liberal Republicanism in England.* Cambridge: Cambridge University Press, 2004.

Taviani, Carlo. *The Making of the Modern Corporation: The Casa di San Giorgio and its Legacy (1446–1720).* New York: Routledge, 2022.

Vergara, Camila. *Systemic Corruption: Constitutional Ideas for an Antioligarchic Republic.* Princeton, NJ: Princeton University Press, 2020.

Wood, Neal. "The Value of Asocial Sociability: Contributions of Machiavelli, Sidney, and Montesquieu." *Bucknell Review* 16 (1968): 1–22.

Wootton, David. *Power, Pleasure, and Profit: Insatiable Appetites from Machiavelli to Madison.* Cambridge, MA: Harvard University Press, 2018.

Zwierlein, Cornel. *"Discorso" und "Lex Dei": die Entstehung neuer Denkrahmen im 16. Jahrhundert und die Wahrnehmung der französischen Religionskriege in Italien und Deutschland.* Gottingen: Vandenhoeck & Ruprecht, 2006.

Index

Sparta, 85, 95, 152; army, 104;
    expansion and defeat, 89,
    95–96, 104, 106–8; institutions,
    89, 92, 103–4, 106–8, 167; social
    concord, 89, 106–7, 167
Spinoza, Baruch, 171, 177
Stalin, Joseph (Iosif Vissarionovich
    Dzhugashvili), 198, 205
state (stato), as a political
    organization, ix, 5, 25, 35, 40–41,
    50–51, 54, 56–58, 70, 73, 94,
    101–2, 107–8, 112–15, 119, 151, 161,
    179–80, 186–88, 190, 192–96,
    205–6, 208. See also community
state (stato), as a condition, 41, 43,
    49–51, 74
Sternberger, Dolf, 201
Stoicism, 36. See also Cicero, Marcus
    Tullius; Seneca, Lucius Annaeus
Strauss, Leo, 201–2, 208–9
Strozzi, Lorenzo, 129, 136
Strozzi family, 12–13, 109
Sulla Felix, Lucius Cornelius, 97,
    100, 109, 113, 147
Syracuse, 46, 48
Swiss. See Switzerland
Switzerland, 2, 25, 85, 189, 200;
    army, 27, 135, 140

Tacitus, Publius Cornelius, 77, 94,
    156, 178–79
Tarquin the Proud (Lucius
    Tarquinius Superbus, king of
    Rome), 55, 121, 133

Tarugi, Francesco, 128
Terence (Publius Terentius Afer),
    20–22, 129–30
Terraferma, 3. See also Venice
Thebes, 95
Theseus (king of Athens), 46
Third Reich, 197, 199–201
Thomas Aquinas, Saint, 181
threats. See passions, fear
Thucydides, 20, 77
time. See necessity; occasion
Tocqueville, Alexis Henri Charles
    de Clérel, count de, 152, 191
Tommasini, Oreste, 192
Tordesillas, Treaty of, 6
totalitarianism, ix, 195, 205. See also
    fascism; Soviet Union; Third
    Reich
Trastámara family. See Aragonese
    family
Treitschke, Heinrich Gothard
    von, 194
Trent, Council of, 133, 173
Trivellato, Francesca, xiii
Tullus Hostilius (king of Rome),
    101, 107
Turks. See Ottoman Empire
Tuscany, 2, 12, 32, 95, 163
Two Sicilies, Kingdom of the, 189

Umbria, 31
United States, 200–201, 203. See
    also under conflict, internal;
    Machiavelli, Niccolò, reception